Specialized Studies in American History Series
Under the General Editorship of:
Robin W. Winks
Fred H. Stopsky
Stanley S. Seaberg
Robert F. Madgic

D0111951

The Woman
in American
History

Gerda Lerner

Sarah Lawrence College

 Addison-Wesley Publishing Company

Menlo Park, California • Reading, Massachusetts • Don Mills, Ontario • London

GERDA LERNER

B.A., New School for Social Research, 1963; M.A., Columbia University, 1965; Ph.D., Columbia University, 1966. Associate professor in history, Sarah Lawrence College, Bronxville, New York, 1968– ; associate professor in history, Long Island University, Greenvale, New York, 1965–68; instructor, New School for Social Research, New York, New York, 1963–1965. Author: articles, short stories, and *The Grimké Sisters from South Carolina: Rebels against Slavery, No Farewell, Black Like Me* (screenplay).

The author and publisher wish to thank the following for granting permission to reproduce the illustrations included in this book.

Amistad Research Center, The Mary McLeod Bethune Papers for the photo on page 121

The Bettmann Archive, Inc., for the photos on pages 25, 43, 136, 168

Boston Public Library for the photo on page 109

Brown Brothers for the photos on pages 74, 78, 151, 179

The Christian Science Publishing Society for the photo on page 148

The Franklin D. Roosevelt Library for the photo on page 174

Historical Pictures Service-Chicago for the photos on pages 13, 36, 97, 113, 156, 166

Hull House, photograph by Wallace Kirkland for the photo on page 127

Library of Congress for the photos on pages 69, 89

Miriam Y. Holden Library for the photos on pages 51, 111, 161

New-York Historical Society for the photo on page 36

Schomburg Collection, New York Public Library for the photo on page 100

Smith College Library, Sophia Smith Collection, Harrison Papers for the photo on page 78

Underwood & Underwood for the photos on pages 56, 181

United Press International for the photos on pages 166, 181,

Wide World Photos for the photos on pages 176, 185

Jane Wright for the photo on page 181

CONTENTS

INTRODUCTION

The role of women in American history has long been ignored. "From reading history in textbooks one would think half of our population made only a negligible contribution to history," wrote the eminent historian, Arthur Schlesinger, Sr., in 1922. Since then there has been little change. This neglect on the part of historians is certainly not an intentional slight. Rather, it has to do with the way historical thinking has developed. For many centuries only kings and military leaders were regarded as fit subjects for historical writing. Then, in the nineteenth century, political leaders and businessmen shared the spotlight. Women had been traditionally excluded from the seats of power. Thus, with the exception of queens, they were excluded from the history texts. With the development of social history other groups previously ignored, such as working people and minorities, began to be studied by historians. Women, too, were now being included, but only in a limited way. Their struggle for legal rights and for suffrage was the only part of their story that seemed worth telling.

Yet, as historian Mary Beard was to point out, women have for centuries been a "force in history." It is time to set the record straight. Women have a history worth knowing. Their contributions, their position in society, and the way society has looked upon them are all part of our social heritage. Besides, women of the past have faced essentially the same problems as do modern women. The way they solved these problems, the various institutions they built, and the ideas they developed about the world and their place in it are part of the background of our own time. In understanding this background better, we learn to understand ourselves and our society better.

Both men and women play multiple *roles* in life. Men play different roles as workers, fathers, and members of a religious or ethnic group. In addition, a man may have one function in a given social group at one time, and a totally different one at another time.

Similarly women, now and in the past, have played different roles as homemakers, workers, and citizens. To describe these different roles, we distinguish between women's social, marital, economic, and legal-political *status*. We shall describe women's status at different points in our history, examine how and why it has changed and analyze the significance of these changes. We shall discuss the contributions of outstanding women, but shall be equally concerned with tracing the ways in which ordinary women have contributed to the American quest for freedom, security, and abundance. If history has heroes, it also has heroines. More significant than isolated individuals, however, are the forces exerted by groups of people having similar concerns and needs. One such force, a significant and generally constructive one, has been the force of women in American history.

PART ONE

The Colonial Period and the American Revolution

Part One

The Colonial Period and
the American Revolution

Women in the American colonies lived under British law, with British traditions of female subordination, and in the traditional male-dominated family. The underlying assumption of colonial society was that the subordinate position of women was natural, sanctioned by tradition and religion, and beneficial to society as a whole. Yet, from the start, the American environment had a liberating influence on women.

The American colonies were economically underdeveloped and suffered from a constant shortage of labor. As in all frontier and developing regions it required the labor and effort of all members of the community—men, women, children, even the aged—merely to survive. The chief occupations of women of all classes were bearing and raising large numbers of children and, within the household, processing whatever food and goods were essential to the family's existence. But there were also considerable numbers of propertied women, planters and managers of large estates. Women were to be found in many businesses and in every kind of trade. They performed an essential economic function in colonial America, and had a much wider range of economic opportunities than women in the Old Country. Frontier conditions created a spirit of comradeship and mutual help, and men and women worked together on a basis of equality, even though law and custom decreed otherwise.

There was, throughout the colonial period, a marked shortage of women, which varied with the regions and was always greatest in the frontier areas. This favorable sex ratio (number of men to number of women in the population) enhanced women's status and position, allowing them greater personal freedom even within the restraints of discriminatory law. All foreign observers of the American colonies remarked on the self-confidence, independent spirit, and dignity of American women.

American courts stretched the letter and spirit of British law to allow women greater latitude in marriage contracts, divorce proceedings, and court settlements. British practice was followed unchanged in the denial of higher education to women, but it must be remembered that higher education was available only to a very small number of upper class young men. In the broad mass of the population a low level of education and literacy prevailed for both sexes.

Women made a considerable contribution to colonial life as community builders and in the creation and maintenance of such institutions as churches, schools, benevolent societies, and charitable organizations. A few talented individuals rose to positions of eminence, but all colonial women enjoyed high status and respect, despite existing discrimination in laws, customs, and educational opportunities.

CHAPTER ONE

The Colonial Woman

Women in colonial America enjoyed greater freedom than did women in contemporary Europe, yet their ability to determine their own lives was limited then, as it is now, by the ideas society held concerning the position of women.

Social Status

The average girl growing up in colonial America lived on an isolated farm or in a small village. More likely than not, she was a member of a large family. Nine was an average family size in New England, and many families had fifteen or more children. Frequently grandparents and unmarried aunts lived in the home. By the time she was ten, the girl would have attended the births and, most likely, the deaths of some of her brothers and sisters. Deaths of children in infancy were frequent, as were the deaths of mothers in childbirth. A girl learned early to assume responsibility for the younger children and to run a household.

Education. In colonial America the education of children was the responsibility of the family. Parents taught their children the most rudimentary skills as best they could. The

11

wealthy educated their sons, and often their daughters, by private tutors. For the poor some writing, enough reading to decipher the Bible, and a few figures were all the education considered necessary.

A girl's education was usually limited to the simplest skills, even in Massachusetts where, as early as 1647, each community was required to set up a public school. At first girls were admitted only during summer sessions, while boys were helping with farm work. Later they attended regular sessions, but their education ended after grammar school. Governor Winthrop of Massachusetts expressed the prevailing opinion when he advised girls to stick to a knowledge of household matters and refrain from "meddling in such things as are proper for the men whose minds are stronger." Another authority thought that girls needed only "sufficient geography to find their way around the house" and "enough chemistry to keep the pot boiling."

Marriage.   In seventeenth century society marriage was the only acceptable career for a girl. The lot of the spinster was unenviable. Unless she had property, she was forced to live out her life as unpaid household help in the home of one of her male relatives. She enjoyed none of the respect and authority of a married or widowed woman. The American colonies were considered "a paradise for women" precisely because here there were so few old maids. In New England there were three times as many men as women; in Virginia, six times. Marriage was possible for every woman who wanted it. Dowries were unnecessary, and even poor girls had their pick of suitable husbands. Widows often remarried a few months after their husband's death.

While the colonial girl knew she would have no trouble finding a husband, that did not mean that she was necessarily free to choose her mate herself. She did have much greater freedom than her European sisters to associate with young men before marriage. Chaperons were seldom in evidence; foreign travelers in America were impressed by the self-assured and "free" attitude of American girls. Still, marriages were a family matter. Wealthy families, in particular, selected their children's marriage partners not so much with personal as with property

12

considerations in mind. However, it was easy for anyone to get free land on the frontier, and young couples who did not agree with their families' decisions had no difficulty in eloping with the partner of their choice.

Once married, the relative freedom of the American girl ceased. The majority of girls married in their teens and, with children coming regularly once a year, soon found their entire time absorbed by their households. Hard work made women age early. Frequent childbirths without medical care and proper rest left many of them with chronic ailments, so much so that painful "female disabilities" were considered a normal aspect of a woman's life. Colonial women could expect to die before their husbands. Gravestones in old churchyards tell a touching story of the fate of colonial wives. One frequently finds the husband living to a ripe old age, surviving several wives and many of his children.

Law. Even in marriage American women were better off than their contemporaries in Europe. Under British law a married woman merged her legal identity with that of her husband.

Her property became her husband's, her earnings, even her clothes belonged to him. She could not sign a contract and could not sue in court; on the other hand, she could not be sued and her husband was fully liable for her debts.

American courts were more lenient toward women. Colonial authorities protected a wife's rights in her husband's property, allowing her a share and her personal clothing in case of a legal separation. Colonial courts also gave women the right to make contracts, transact business, and sue during their husband's absence. Most important, they upheld premarital contracts between husband and wife in regard to the wife's property. While these became an accepted instrument by which wealthy women could retain property rights, the majority of women had no such protection.

Women in America, as well as in Britain, suffered under severe legal disabilities. The husband was the sole guardian over the children, even in case of divorce. He could dispose of his wife's earnings at will and squander her inherited property. His authority over the home was absolute, and wife and children were without protection if he abused his power. Divorces were seldom granted. The one recourse abused wives had was to run away and, judging from the frequent advertisements for runaway wives in colonial newspapers, they availed themselves of the opportunity quite freely. Running away was practicable because, due to the constant labor shortage in the American colonies, women could always find work. Therefore the American environment enabled women on the whole to enjoy more freedom than the letter of the law allowed. The following advertisement by Sarah Cantwell of South Carolina is quite atypical, but the advertisement illustrates the independent spirit of some colonial women:

> John Cantwell has the impudence to advertise me in the Papers, cautioning all Persons against crediting me; he never had any Credit till he married me; As for his Bed and Board mentioned, he had neither Bed nor Board when he married me; I never eloped, I went away before his face when he beat me.[1]

Economic Status

Colonial America was an underdeveloped country; it could not afford the luxury of idle hands. Besides, Protestant religious doctrine supported the belief that idleness was sinful. Therefore, work for women, married or single, was regarded as a civic and religious duty. Puritan town councils expected single girls and widows to be self-supporting and provided needy spinsters with parcels of land to farm. Wives were expected to help their husbands in their trade and continue it in case of widowhood. Children, too, were expected to do their share. Those over six years of age helped on the family farm or were apprenticed to learn some trade. Needy children, girls as well as boys, had to work for their keep.

Servants. Men and women who migrated to America as servants had no difficulty in finding work. These indentured servants usually contracted their services to a master for a period of five to seven years. At the end of the contract time they received their freedom and some wages. Children indentured into service received their freedom when they reached their teens. If a servant was found guilty of any misdeed, he was usually punished by a lengthening of his term of service. In this regard women were somewhat worse off than men. If the violation called for a fine, women, who had less chance of earning cash wages, were often unable to pay the fine and were punished by whipping. If a servant girl had an illegitimate child her term of service was lengthened, while the man in the case usually went unpunished. Still, the favorable prospects for marriage and employment made life in the colonies very attractive for poor women, many of whom came to America to improve their position.

Household Industry. The vast majority of colonial women worked in their homes, in activities absolutely essential to the survival of their families. Whatever their husbands and sons produced from field and forest, women processed. In addition to supplying the essential needs of their families, many women managed to produce a surplus of one or another of their products for sale. Thus the entire colonial production of cloth and

15

clothing and, to a lesser extent, of shoes, was in the hands of women.

Work Outside the Home. Besides these household occupations, women also found employment in a great variety of other trades. They were butchers, silversmiths, gunsmiths, and upholsterers. They ran mills, tanneries, shipyards, and every kind of shop, tavern, and boardinghouse. They were gate keepers, jail keepers, sextons, journalists, printers, doctoresses, apothecaries, midwives, nurses, and teachers. Women acquired their skills in the same way men did—through apprenticeship training, frequently within their own families. Many women learned their trade from their husband and continued their husband's business when they were widowed. Thus Dianah Nuthead of Maryland became a printer. After their respective husbands' deaths, Elizabeth Timothy became owner and publisher of the *South Carolina Gazette,* and Anne Green of the *Maryland Gazette.* The widow of printer John Peter Zenger carried on his publishing business in New York City.

Women made an important contribution to colonial society in caring for the sick and disabled. Colonial America had no medical schools, few hospitals, and no laws licensing doctors or medical workers. Clergymen, governors, barbers, quacks, apprentices, and women all practiced medicine. Most practitioners acquired their skill by reading a few medical volumes and serving an apprenticeship with an established practitioner. Among these "physics"—surgeons and healers—the occasional doctoress was fully accepted and often well rewarded. County records of all the colonies contain references to the work of these female physicians. There was even an army physician, a Mrs. Allyn, who served during King Philip's war. Plantation records name several slave women who were granted special privileges because of their useful service as medical practitioners. Women also played an important role as primitive apothecaries, collecting herbs and brewing them into healing potions and liniments. And nearly every woman at some time served as a nurse for members of her family and for neighbors. The laying out of the dead and their preparation for burial was also the responsibility of women.

Women held a monopoly of the profession of midwifery. There are many records of well trained midwives with diplomas from European institutions who successfully served in America. In most colonies midwives were licensed, examined before a board, and registered.

Proprietors. Many women were planters and managers of large estates. Deborah Moody, a large landowner in Salem, Massachusetts, left that colony in 1643 with a group of dissenters for the Dutch colony of New Netherland. As the first woman to receive a colonial land grant, she founded Gravesend, Long Island, planned the township, invited settlers, set up and managed the community on the principle of religious toleration for all faiths, and defended it successfully against an attack by Indians.

Other important colonial land owners were the two Brent sisters, each of whom owned and developed a "manor" of over one thousand acres in Maryland. As owners of manorial estates, the sisters Brent had the right to hold "court-baron," feudal court sessions in which they dispensed justice. Mistress Margaret Brent not only managed her large plantations, but brought suit in court and appeared as legal spokesman for other gentlewomen. She was so respected that Governor Calvert named her as the executor of his will. After his death she exerted considerable influence in the political affairs of the colony, once even settling a soldiers' mutiny. In 1647 she asked for the right to be seated and to vote in the Maryland Assembly—the first woman in America to ask for the vote and for political office. She received the right to vote in her capacity as Governor Calvert's attorney but was not seated in the Assembly.

Eliza Lucas Pinckney (1723–1793). The wives and daughters of southern planters carried considerable responsibilities in the running and management of the plantations. Outstanding among these women was Eliza Lucas Pinckney, who made a major contribution to the economic life of the Carolinas. While her father was on tour of duty as the royal governor of Antigua, seventeen-year-old Eliza took over the full management of his plantations near Charleston. "I have the business of three plantations to transact," she noted in her diary in 1740 and went on to describe a series of remarkable agricultural experiments. At that time rice was the Carolinas' prime agricultural commodity. Eliza experimented methodically with different crops, hoping to find a better export product, and at last settled on indigo (a seed used for the making of a dye). After long and tedious trials, she finally developed a marketable seed and began to introduce it to other planters. Indigo soon became the second biggest export staple of the Carolinas, contributing considerably to the area's economic growth. Eliza also experimented with other agricultural products, planting oaks for sale as lumber, growing and drying figs for export, shipping food to the army in Antigua, and pickling eggs in brine. With all this she managed daily to study some Plutarch and Virgil, to read French, and to practice shorthand. She instructed her little sisters and the Negro children of her plantation in reading, practiced the piano, and did needlework.

When her father tried to arrange a marriage, giving her the choice of two gentlemen, she answered politely but firmly:

> Honoured Sir . . . . As you propose Mr. L to me I am sorry I can't have Sentiments favourable enough to him to take time to think on the Subject . . . . But as I know 'tis my Happiness you consult, I must beg the favour of you to pay my compliments to the old Gentleman for his Generosity and favourable sentiments and let him know . . . that the riches of Chili and Peru put together if he had them, could not purchase a sufficient Esteem for him to make him my husband.[2]

As to the other gentleman, she had insufficient acquaintance with him and besides, she pointed out, she was only eighteen and wished to remain single for at least another three years. She signed the letter "Your most dutiful and Affectionate daughter." Her father did not insist and much later Eliza Lucas chose her own husband, a widower of a distinguished family, Charles Pinckney, who became chief justice of South Carolina in 1758. Her sons, Charles Cotesworth and Thomas, were both leaders in the American Revolution, one becoming governor of South

Carolina, the other the United States' minister to England. This remarkable woman was greatly respected in her lifetime. A year before her death President George Washington went out of his way on his trip to South Carolina to greet and honor her publicly.

CHAPTER TWO

Dissenters and Community Builders

The underlying assumption of colonial society was that women ought to occupy an inferior and subordinate position. The settlers had brought this idea with them from Europe. It was reflected in their legal concepts, their willingness to exclude women from political life, and their discriminatory educational practices. Most women accepted the position men had established for them, and lived quiet lives at home. Those few outstanding women, such as Margaret Brent and Eliza Lucas Pinckney, who ignored many of the restrictions placed on colonial women, were exceptional.

Another small group of exceptional women consisted of those who dared rebel against a woman's established place in religious affairs.

Dissenters

Women in the Massachusetts Bay colony were expected to follow the teachings of the leaders of the Protestant Reformation, who were unanimous in demanding the subordination of women both in home and church. John Knox spoke for all of them, "Woman in her greatest perfection, was made to serve and obey man, not to rule and command him. . . . After her fall and rebellion committed against God . . . she was made subject to men by the irrevocable sentence of God." If further authority was needed, the ministers quoted Saint Paul. "Let women keep silence in the congregation, for it is not permitted to them to speak, but to be subject as the law sayeth."

Societal strictures against "meddling women" and the belief that women should not speak publicly in church affairs explain, in part, the particular severity with which Massachusetts dealt with the religious dissenter, Anne Hutchinson.

Anne Hutchinson (1589[?]–1643).   Anne Hutchinson was the first in the New World to challenge the dogma of women's subordination to men. A member of a highly respected merchant family, she came to the Massachusetts Bay colony in 1634. Of her fifteen children, three had died in England and two were born in America. Highly respected for her knowledge of midwifery and herbal healing, Anne Hutchinson enjoyed the friendship of the leading minister, John Cotton. However, she soon scandalized the leaders of the colony by her habit of gathering women in her home to comment on and interpret scripture.

Anne Hutchinson preached the religious freedom of the individual conscience, the revelation of God's grace without the necessity of following the interpretation of the learned ministry, and the possibility of salvation by a sincere "feeling" of conversion. In Puritan Massachusetts such views threatened to undermine the authority of church and state. Anne Hutchinson was brought to trial by the civil court and by the church. Both courts found her guilty of heresy and ordered her banished from the colony. When she and her family fled to the more tolerant climate of Roger Williams' colony in Rhode Island, thirty-five other families followed. The little group later migrated once more to the shores of Long Island Sound, where in 1643 Anne Hutchinson and most of her family were killed by the Indians.

Mary Dyer (-?–1660).   During Anne Hutchinson's trial in Massachusetts, only one hand was raised in her defense—that

21

of Mary Dyer, who later became a dissenter herself. Mary Dyer joined the Quakers and challenged the authorities of the Bay colony by attempting to preach her new faith in Massachusetts.

This was at a time when the colony had punished Quakers, many women among them, by whippings, imprisonment, and deportation. Mary Dyer witnessed to her faith, defying increasingly severe sentences. In 1659 she was sentenced to death in Boston, together with two male Quakers. She watched their execution, was prepared for her own, and reprieved at the last minute due to popular pressure. She was banished from the colony once again, but returned the next year with the deliberate intent of challenging the savage persecution of her co-religionists. This time there was no reprieve, and she was hanged from the gallows on April 1, 1660.

The dissenters, among them Roger Williams, Anne Hutchinson, and Mary Dyer, contributed to the weakening of Puritan orthodoxy and to the later development of religious tolerance. More significantly, Anne Hutchinson, the first woman to preach to women, asserted the right of women to participate in religious affairs on a basis of equality. In this she was a woman far ahead of her time. Two other women, Ann Lee and Jemima Wilkinson, became founders of religious sects, but their following was insignificant.

During colonial times all the major religious groups relegated women to the role of silent participation in church affairs, and none admitted them to the ministry. The only exception was the Society of Friends, known as the Quakers. They believed in the equality of men and women before God and gave boys and girls the same education, and adults of both sexes the same opportunity to speak at their worship services. From the ranks of Quakers came some of the leaders of the feminist movement in the nineteenth century.

Community Builders

Next in importance to the economic function of colonial women, discussed in Chapter One, was their contribution to the building of communities. As one historian has said, "The participation of women in every sphere of life and labor was absolutely imperative to the success of the American colonies." The Spaniards settled their colonies with soldiers, missionaries, and adventurers, as did the French. In both cases these largely male settlements were outposts for exploitation of the colonies rather than communities. It was the bringing of white women to the British colonies that altered the character of the British settlements. Whether housed in a primitive dugout shelter, a sod lean-to, or a log cabin, women attempted to recreate the life of the Old Country in the wilderness. Anthropologists refer to women as being "culture carriers," whose function it is to transmit the inheritance of culture to the growing child and the environment. Thus, pioneer women were essential not only to the survival of their families but to the building of communities in the New World.

Frontier Life.   Pioneer settlers, hunters, and ranchers were generally eager to move westward to better land as soon as their exploitative methods of agriculture had exhausted the soil. This kind of life was hard on women, who tended to exert what influence they could toward the formation of permanent communities. Because of scouting and hunting expeditions and frequent family moves, the men of the family were sometimes absent for long periods of time, during which the women had to fend for themselves and their households. This meant not only coping with the usual hardships of wilderness farming, but often defending crops, farm, and lives against attacking Indians. There are many instances of great heroism by women in such situations. Most famous of all women fighters was Hannah Dustin, who in 1697 was captured by Indians and, with another woman and a boy, killed her ten Indian captors while they were asleep and escaped to her home.

No matter how scattered the settlements in the frontier region were, women found a way of helping a neighbor in childbirth, illness or death. Quilting bees and other simple social occasions soon led to the formation of community institutions. The first of these usually were churches. Women played an important part in the establishment of churches, not only by their insistence on bringing husband and children to the church services on Sunday, but by their organization of financial support over and above the tithing. These informal fundraising activities later developed into organized church and missionary societies.

Frontier life was difficult, but it instilled in men and women a spirit of self-reliance, courage, and resourcefulness. Since much of colonial life was frontier life, many colonial women shared in this kind of experience. The frail woman who demanded chivalrous protection and expensive luxuries was the exception in colonial America. Even the wealthy upper-class ladies of the colonies were actively involved in the life of their communities and the affairs of their husbands and sons.

The War for Independence

In the War for Independence women played a role of considerable significance. Many were enthusiastic supporters of the idea of independence. From socially prominent Abigail Adams, wife of future President John Adams, to the humblest New England farm wife, women encouraged their men to stand fast and did all they could to support them. Long before the outbreak of hostilities they pledged themselves to boycott British goods, especially tea. Once the fighting started, they effectively supported the war on the home front. One woman writing from Philadelphia spoke for many:

> I have retrenched every superfluous expense in my table and family. Tea I have not drunk since last Christmas, nor bought a new cap or gown since your defeat at Lexington; and, what I never did before, have learned to knit, and am now making stockings of wool for my servants; and this way do I throw in my mite to the public good. I know this, that as free I can die but once; but as a slave I shall not be worthy of life.[3]

Other women curbed war speculators and joined the "Daughters of Liberty" and similar patriotic organizations. One

24

Molly Pitcher, Revolutionary heroine

of their major contributions was to organize and provide care for the wounded. They made shirts and clothing for the soldiers, collected and shipped hospital supplies, and set up efficient networks of relief organizations. The first of these was organized in Philadelphia by Esther Reed and Sarah Franklin Bache, the daughter of Benjamin Franklin. More than 1600 women heeded the appeal of the ladies' relief organization and collected the equivalent of $7500 in gold to buy supplies for the soldiers. The women of New Jersey, South Carolina, and Massachusetts organized similar campaigns.

War Work. During the war women took over men's jobs, wove and spun material for soldiers' clothing, and outfitted the home front with "homespun" garments. They did the heavy work of farming, collected lead, which was in short supply, and made it into bullets. Women worked in arms manufacturing and supplied the armies in the field. At times they themselves took up guns. Two women, Sally St. Clair of South Carolina and Deborah Sampson of Massachusetts, dressed up as men and served as soldiers. The well-known Molly Pitcher was not alone in replacing her man on the firing line. Margaret Corbin

was honored by Congress with a soldier's pension for filling the artillery post of her husband, who was killed by her side.

Soldiers were poorly and irregularly paid during the American Revolution, and there were no family allotments. Women willingly bore these hardships for the sake of their country. Some performed heroic feats to save their crops from enemy troops, and others acted as couriers and spies for the Continental Army.

Mercy Otis Warren (1728–1814). A unique contribution to the American Revolution was made by Mercy Otis Warren, sister of James Otis. This brilliant woman had the advantage of sharing a good education with her brothers. She carried on extensive correspondence with the outstanding minds of her time, was a close friend of John and Abigail Adams, and is believed to have been as instrumental as her brother James in setting up the Committees of Correspondence. These were important for rousing and organizing the scattered revolutionary forces before the outbreak of the war. Mercy Otis Warren was a poet and the author of three satirical plays, which ridiculed the British and the Tories and were very popular. The mother of five sons, she found time to write two tragedies and several pamphlets and, in 1805, to publish a three volume history of the American Revolution.

Yet talented women of achievement like Mercy Otis Warren, Abigail Adams, and Eliza Pinckney were few and far between in colonial America. Not until the American Revolution broadened economic and educational opportunities were ordinary women able to aspire to the privileges of the few.

PART TWO

From the Birth of the Republic to the Civil War

The period from the American Revolution to the Civil War was one of tremendous change in American society. The building of turnpikes, canals, and later railroads led to a revolution in agriculture and commerce, and spurred westward migration and the growth of cities. Women shared in the benefits of increasing wealth, urbanization and industrialization. Middle-class women of the eastern seaboard now could enjoy a longer period of education and more leisure time. They could become "ladies," a rank formerly reserved for wealthy women only. Their cultural needs were served by the development of mass circulation magazines. These, in turn, gave rise to a new generation of literary women whose influence on their culture was significant.

With these developments came drastic changes in the ideas society held about the place, the role, and the work of women. As the "lady" started to become an ideal of true womanhood, the idea that "woman's place is in the home" and nowhere else began to be widely accepted. At the same time, due to the licensing of many professions, women were excluded from fields and businesses in which they had formerly been active. This narrowing of woman's "proper sphere" had an adverse impact on middle-class women. It contributed to the feelings of frustration of an educated elite which would later lead to an organized movement for woman's rights.

The lives of wealthy and poor women were now more differentiated than ever before. At the time when employment and professional opportunities for middle-class women were narrowed, the poorer women found new occupations through industrialization. New England factories depended on the labor of women and children. The increasing shortage of male teachers in the New England states brought women as a group into the teaching field.

There were some improvements in the property rights of women before the Civil War, but these only benefited the wealthy few. Women participated in the various reform movements of the Ante-Bellum period, first in separate organizations, and later demanding to take part on a basis of equality in all the major reforms. The discrimination they experienced in the course of these efforts gave impetus to the formation of the woman's rights movement. While legally the political status of women had remained unchanged, the relative advances made by men in electoral participation during the Jacksonian era made some women more keenly aware of their disadvantaged position.

The Ante-Bellum period, then, was for women one of spreading educational and economic opportunities with simultaneous frustrations and increasing restraints. It was a period of change and tension leading to new ideas, new demands, new organizations. Between the American Revolution and the Civil War, American society produced the conditions which would lead women to organize in a struggle for their greater freedom.

CHAPTER THREE

Ladies and "Scribbling Women"

The American Revolution had written the concept of equality into the Constitution and set the nation on the road to increasing egalitarianism. Privilege based on ability rather than on inheritance, freedom of the individual, and opportunities of economic advancement for all groups of society had now become the stated goals, if not always the realities, of American society. After the American Revolution, the proposition that all men were created equal became transformed into a political promise: "If all men are not actually equal, they should be." It was inevitable that, sooner or later, women would ask: "If all men are created equal, why not women?"

Equality of Opportunity

In the early nineteenth century, however, "equality" was generally accepted to mean "equal opportunity"—an equal chance to rise in the world, an equal chance to share in the nation's abundance, an equal chance to have access to power. For women, who had never had direct access to power, this meant simply a chance to elevate their own and their families' status. Urban families and those enjoying increasingly higher standards of living were able to afford the time and expense necessary to provide their daughters with a more "refined" education. The female academies in and around eastern cities served this need and prepared the girls for favorable marriages. A smattering of French, a bit of religious reading, the ability to write a fine hand and recite some uplifting verse, embroidery, sketching, a little dancing, and enough skill on the piano to entertain family and guests with a few selections—these were considered sufficient "accomplishments" for a young lady. Once married, a lady had to follow the fashions, adorn her home so as to display her husband's wealth to best advantage, and help raise her family's cultural standards. In this pursuit the ladies' magazines were of significant help.

Morals and Manners

Ladies' Magazines. In 1792 the first *All Lady Repository* appeared, to be followed by an increasing number of magazines addressed to women. By the 1840's, these magazines had reached mass circulation. They transmitted the latest information regarding fashions, popular science, household hints, and stories which were little more than fictionalized tracts. They preached through sentimental poetry and equally sentimental fiction the "culture of true womanhood." Piety, purity, and domesticity were the foundations on which to build feminine happiness. The heroine of fiction practiced all of these virtues and found contentment in woman's only proper sphere, the home.

By teaching every woman proper standards of behavior, dress, and literary tastes, mass circulation magazines fostered the aspirations of lower-class women who wanted to become ladies as much as did middle-class women. This unending stream of printed matter demanded an army of writers. Who better than women could find the proper tone and approach? A host of "scribbling women" began to influence the literary scene.

The female writers of popular literature shared the background and tastes of their audiences. The first novel written in the United States was authored by Sarah Wentworth in 1781. Hannah Foster's *The Coquette,* a sentimental piece published in 1797, ran through thirteen editions. Susanna Rowson's *Charlotte Temple,* a hackneyed "vice-does-not-pay" story, enchanted generations of faithful readers. But female writers only began to come into their own with the advent of ladies' magazines.

Contributions to these magazines were at first submitted anonymously. By the 1830's it was possible for a lady to admit to authorship. Lydia Sigourney enchanted tens of thousands of readers with her imitative, saccharine poetry and, burdened with an incompetent husband, managed to support her family for years on her literary earnings. Sarah Josepha Hale, best known to posterity as the author of *Mary Had a Little Lamb,* exerted tremendous influence through her forty years as literary editor of *Godey's Lady's Book,* the most important magazine of its type, with a circulation of 150,000. Mrs. Hale, a firm advocate of refined taste and pure morals, was also a woman of practical good sense. She used her columns to advocate higher education for women and to advise their training as doctors and nurses, occupations she considered perfectly compatible with "true womanhood." A prolific writer, editor, and compiler, she published a total of thirty-six volumes during her lifetime and inspired other women to take up journalistic careers.

Two other successful ladies' magazines of the period, *Graham's* and *Peterson's,* were edited by men, but there were several reform journals edited and staffed entirely by women. Some were devoted to the causes of temperance and antislavery, others to health and hygiene.

Dress Reform.   Amelia Bloomer, deputy postmistress of Seneca Falls, New York, was one of those who advanced from moderate reform to more radical causes. In 1849, when she became the timid editor of a temperance journal, appropriately called *The Lily,* she had no intention of doing anything more than exhorting her readers to abstain from drunkenness and debauchery. Since most of her readers were ladies like herself, these exhortations were quite unnecessary. A few years later, her friend Elizabeth Miller became an ardent advocate of dress reform and persuaded Mrs. Bloomer to advance the cause of a "Turkish costume," first worn in America by the unconventional British actress Fanny Kemble. Mrs. Bloomer, soon persuaded of the advantages of pantaloons gathered chastely at the ankles and topped by a belted smock which reached the knees, took up the cause. Daringly she rushed into print with the assertion that women "maintain that we have the right to control our . . . wardrobe." This at a time when the New York *Herald* declared, "the attempt to introduce pantaloons . . . will not succeed. Those who have tried it, will very likely soon end their career in the lunatic asylum, or perchance, in the state prison." The New York *Courier and Enquirer* cautioned, "Nothing could sooner break down our respect for woman" than the attempt to shed her fashionable costume of fifteen pounds of whalebone, bustles, petticoats, and heavy skirts. The objection was based on the threat of "notoriety and . . . the broad glare of publicity. The sun belongs to man, the shade is woman's. Notoriety is the foul fiend at whose feet she falls and perishes."

For Mrs. Bloomer "notoriety" meant that her name became synonymous with the very garment she had so prematurely endorsed. Forgotten as a temperance reformer, Mrs. Bloomer went down in history as a dress reformer, even though her cause did not succeed until after the achievement of most other reforms demanded by women.

Literary Careers

The women who took up professional literary pursuits, somewhat derisively dubbed by Nathaniel Hawthorne "that mob of scribbling women," had in common with men who took up similar careers their talent, drive, and economic need. Unlike most women of their time, they came from families in which they had enjoyed an unusually good education. A large proportion of them were single or widowed, and many of them had dependents to support. Their career choices, unlike those of literary men, were limited. They could not become doctors, lawyers, or ministers; except for teaching, writing was the only professional career available to a lady in the middle of the nineteenth century.

Lydia Maria Child (1802–1880). A popular novelist, Lydia Maria Child pioneered in establishing a children's magazine in 1827. Her household hint book, *The Frugal Housewife,* went into twenty editions in seven years and was followed by her *Mother's Book,* an encyclopedia on child care. In 1832 she published a history of women, consisting of three volumes of biographies of heroines who seemed to her proper models for American women. This compilation was remarkable as an early expression of feminist interest.

In 1833, when Lydia Maria Child published *An Appeal for that Class of Americans Called Africans,* a lengthy essay against slavery, she cast her lot with the radical abolitionists. Despite the subsequent publication of several novels, she never regained her earlier literary popularity. She became the editor of one of the abolitionist newspapers, *The Anti-Slavery Standard,* and her output continued to be prolific.

Her literary merit was summed up by a friend: "She wrote better than most of her contemporaries and well enough for her public." But Lydia Maria Child's significance lies not so much in her literary career as in her willingness to risk it for the most despised and most radical cause of her day—abolitionism. She reached her largest audience with a pamphlet written in 1860 on behalf of Captain John Brown, then awaiting execution in a Virginia jail. It sold over 300,000 copies.

Louisa May Alcott (1832–1888). The daughter of the idealistic, impractical, and always penniless educator, Bronson Alcott, Louisa May Alcott was driven to writing by her strong desire for independence. As a schoolteacher she could not quite support herself, but as a writer, living in a garret in Boston, she could. "I like the independent feeling," she admitted, "and though it is not an easy life, it is a free one, and I enjoy it." Her *Little Women* and other novels depicted the life of her times with considerable realism, skill, and charming good humor. This combination, plus her ability to delineate character and tell a good story, appealed to audiences then and now and made Louisa May Alcott successful and rich.

Jane Swisshelm (1815–1884).   On the frontier, journalistic opportunities for women were greater than literary opportunities. One of the most colorful journalists of her time was Jane Swisshelm, who owned and edited *The St. Cloud Visiter* [*sic*] in Minnesota. The paper was popular, largely because of its editor's pithy and outspoken comments on any number of controversial subjects of which the following, concerning the supposed intellectual inferiority of women, is an example:

> It is well known that thousands, nay, millions of women in this country are condemned to the most menial drudgery, such as men would scorn to engage in, and that for one

fourth the wages. . . . They plough, harrow, reap, dig . . .
do anything that is hard work, physical labor, and who
says anything against it? But let one presume to use her
mental powers—let her aspire to turn editor, public
speaker, doctor, lawyer . . . O! bring cologne, get a cambric
kerchief and feather fan, unloose his corsets and take off
his cravat! What a fainting fit Mr. Propriety has taken! Just
to think that one of the . . . heavenly angels should forsake
. . . woman's sphere![4]

Her feud with the local Democratic party boss, Sylvanus
Lowry, whom she accused of proslavery sympathies, was a
no-holds-barred affair. Invective was answered with invective,
but the lady editor's ridicule was finally more than the politician could stand. He arranged for some men to break into her
office, destroy her press, and throw the type into the river. A
meeting of local citizens was called to finish the job by forcing
the editor to leave town.

Jane Swisshelm took up the challenge and appeared at the
meeting. She announced that she had made her will and that a
friend of hers was in attendance with a pistol and orders to
"shoot her square through the brain, if there was no other way
of preventing her from falling into the hands of the mob." Her
defiant courage won over the crowd; they even collected money
to replace her press. Mrs. Swisshelm promptly renewed her
denunciation of Lowry, who then brought a $10,000 libel suit
against her. Since she had no money for a long court fight, Mrs.
Swisshelm settled by signing a pledge that her *St. Cloud Visiter*
would never refer to Mr. Lowry again. She kept her word. The
next week she stopped publication of the *St. Cloud Visiter* and
appeared with a new paper, *The Democrat,* in which she repeated all her charges against Lowry and stated, "We have
pledged our honor that the paper we edit will discuss any subject we have in mind to discuss." She was never bothered again
by either politician or mob and continued to delight her readers
by her savage and irrepressible comments.

Harriet Beecher Stowe (1811–1896).   The most famous of
the antislavery writers, Harriet Beecher Stowe wrote magazine

37

(left) Lydia Maria Child
(right) Harriet Beecher Stowe

stories for years in order to supplement the meager family income. She wrote in spare moments while taking care of the needs of her large family, keeping her writing paper in her sewing basket to have it handy. *Uncle Tom's Cabin* was conceived not so much as a novel but as a moral and religious treatise. Impelled by the revulsion she felt over passage of the Fugitive Slave Act, Mrs. Stowe took up her pen determined to bring home to the nation a realization of the horrors of slavery. The story caught hold of her and she wrote at a fever pitch of emotion, publishing the chapters serially in a Washington antislavery magazine. The novel was an immediate and staggering success, selling 2,500,000 copies in the United States and abroad in its first year of publication, 1851. As a popular minstrel play it reached even wider audiences. Few writers of any period could claim as much influence.

Yet even the author of *Uncle Tom's Cabin* had to bear her share of "notoriety" and vilification. Rather than attacking her book, defenders of slavery were unanimous in attacking her integrity and gentility—any woman who dared to write as she had, could not be a lady. To rebut her, at least fourteen novels appeared in defense of slavery. In unwitting tribute to the acceptance of female writers, to which Mrs. Stowe had so largely contributed, most of these were written by women.

The lady editors, writers, and journalists of the early nineteenth century were, as a group, not particularly brave, nor were they consciously pioneering. Most of them simply wanted to earn a decent living. As it happened, they filled a cultural need, opened new careers for women, and affected their contemporaries' outlook on life. That their influence was often overly sentimental, narrowly pious and parochial, tediously uplifting, and snobbishly genteel cannot be ignored. They fashioned popular taste and, at times, corrupted it. But they also reflected with accuracy the taste of their readers, and the best of them worked steadfastly to improve that taste and widen the horizons and interests of American women.

CHAPTER FOUR

Women Leave the Home to Work

In 1783 Lucinda Foote, aged twelve, was examined by a board at Yale College and found "fully qualified, except in her sex, to be received as a pupil of the freshman class of Yale University." The unfortunate Lucinda, thus denied her chance for higher education, thereafter vanished from history. But many other girls with intellectual promise buried their disappointment in the pages of a diary. "Oh, had I received the education I desired, had I been bred to the profession of the law, I might have been a useful member of society," wrote Sarah Grimké, born in 1792.

Education for Women

These cries of disappointment were occasionally translated into calls for action in the reform of women's education. Abigail Adams reminded her husband, President John Adams, of the urgent need for educational reform: "If you complain of education in sons, what shall I say in regard to daughters, who ever experience the want of it? . . . If we mean to have heroes, statesmen and philosophers we should have learned women."

The essayist Judith Sargent Murray questioned whether women's mental faculties were indeed inferior to those of men, as was generally believed in her time. She suggested that the real cause of the different intellectual development of the sexes lay in a different education. "I would calmly ask, is it reasonable, that a candidate for immortality . . . an intelligent being . . . should at present be so degraded as to be allowed no other ideas, than those which are suggested by the mechanics of a pudding, or the sewing of the seams of a garment?" But Mrs. Murray's ideas and those of the other critics remained isolated expressions of advanced thinking until several decades later when Emma Willard, Catherine Beecher, and Mary Lyon joined the two great educators Henry Barnard and Horace Mann in a major reform of American education.

Emma Hart Willard (1787–1870).   After teaching girls in private academies for years, Emma Hart Willard applied for permission to take the state teachers' examination at the University of Middlebury in Vermont. Denied this opportunity simply because she was a woman, she set out to raise the educational standards of female students and teachers without the benefit of a professional degree. In her Middlebury Seminary she subjected young ladies to a rigorous academic program, including such "male" subjects as algebra, trigonometry, history, and geography. She taught herself and her teachers by methods of her own invention and wrote her own textbooks.

Emma Willard was convinced that the education of women would remain inferior as long as it remained private. She tried to gain public support and funds for her seminary but was met by the response, "They will be educating the cows next." But she proved to the scoffers that girls could master difficult theoretical subjects without losing their health, their femininity, or their refinement.

Mrs. Willard's husband, himself an educator, always encouraged her in her work. After the family moved to upstate New York, Emma Willard presented Governor DeWitt Clinton and the legislature of New York with a well-conceived plan for improving female education. In her "Address to the Public," published in 1819, she asked for state aid in founding schools for girls and outlined an ambitious curriculum. With Governor Clinton's endorsement, the legislature voted a charter for her seminary, but would not grant her a subsidy. Mrs. Willard then secured the financial support of the city of Troy, and in 1821 the Troy Female Seminary opened its doors, the first institution in the United States to offer a high school education to girls.

Emma Willard was one of the great educators of her day. After 1838 she turned her attention to improvement of the common schools and worked with Henry Barnard in Connecticut. She correctly appraised the essential role women would play in the development of public education. "I continued to educate teachers until two hundred had gone from the Troy Seminary before one was educated in any public normal school in the United States." The graduates of her seminary went on to spread the gospel of quality education for women across the country. Emma Willard persuaded her pupils that they owed it

to themselves and their country to teach for at least a few years of their lives. Her students became a moving force in the spread of public education.

Frances Wright (1795–1852).   The demand for public education was raised not only by ambitious middle-class parents, but also by mechanics and workingmen, who in 1830 began to organize trade unions and political parties in the eastern cities. They were encouraged and spurred on in their demand for public education, which was very radical for the time, by a brilliant, though erratic Scotswoman. Well educated, attractive, and dedicated to a variety of good causes, Frances Wright had come to America in 1824. She scandalized American propriety as much by her behavior as by her unorthodox opinions. After an unhappy experience in setting up a utopian colony in Tennessee, she had begun a course of public lectures in Ohio, Pennsylvania, and New York. The fact of her lecturing would have been "notorious" enough, but Frances Wright together with Robert Dale Owen edited a magazine addressed to workingmen in which she advocated a variety of radical ideas, including birth control, atheism, and free public education for all people. Of the many causes she embraced, only that of free public education won support from her contemporaries.

Teacher Training

Catherine Beecher (1800–1878).   Connecticut established the first public education system in the United States in 1842. From the start, the need for trained teachers was critical. In this field Catherine Beecher, the daughter of the famous minister Lyman Beecher, found her usefulness. Equipped with an extraordinary mind and a strong will, she raised her eight orphaned brothers and sisters and then, grief-stricken by the death of her fiance and determined to serve society, took up the cause of improving women's education.

By subscription of Hartford residents, she raised the funds necessary to erect a model school building with all the latest equipment. Her teachers each specialized in two or three subjects, in marked contrast to the usual practice whereby teachers attempted to cover as many as twenty different "branches" of education. Her pupils had to take entrance examinations and received diplomas only after passing rigorous tests. Most of them went on to staff the school systems of the western states. Later, she pioneered by setting up teacher training institutions in the West.

Great as were Catherine Beecher's contributions to teacher training, she subscribed to a narrow view of woman's sphere. To her, housewifery and motherhood were the chief functions of a woman's life, and teaching was merely an extension of the childraising function. Her main interest lay in upgrading women's skills to the professional level. She made a large contribution to this by writing a home economics book with her younger sister, Harriet Beecher Stowe, which ran through several editions. This book differed from others of its kind by taking a scientific approach and by offering a knowledge of hygiene, medicine, diet, and plumbing to its readers.

Teaching was a field characterized by a constant and severe shortage of labor. Americans were committed to educating their children in public schools, but they were insistent on doing so as cheaply as possible. Women were available in great numbers and they were willing to work for low wages. Generally, thirty to fifty percent of the wages paid to male teachers seemed appropriate for females. When Susan B. Anthony worked as a schoolteacher, her wages were two dollars a week and board, little more than she had made as a spooler in her father's textile mill.

In 1853, Susan B. Anthony attended a State Teachers Convention in Rochester and listened patiently to hours of debate. The speakers, all men, complained that teachers were regarded without any respect and that their wages were beneath subsistence level. Susan B. Anthony attempted for half an hour to gain the floor. Then finally, with a condescending "the lady may speak," she was permitted to address the gathering:

> None of you quite comprehend the cause of the disrespect of which you complain. Do you not see that so long as society says woman is incompetent to be a lawyer, minister or doctor, but has ample ability to be a teacher, every man of you who chooses this profession tacitly acknowledges that he has no more brains than a woman? And this, too, is the reason that teaching is a less lucrative profession as here men must compete with the cheap labor of woman. ... Would you exalt your profession, exalt those who labor with you ... increase the salary of the women engaged in the noble work of educating our future President, Senators and Congressmen.[5]

At that time Susan B. Anthony's plea fell on deaf ears. The schoolmarm of the nineteenth century did not yet enjoy the dignity of the trained professional. The real step forward was made only when higher education for women became a reality.

Mary Lyon (1797–1849). Dissatisfied with her own inadequate preparation for teaching, Mary Lyon developed a plan for setting up a women's college. After trying to stay in the

44

background and let men do the promotion work, she soon found that she was the best advocate of her cause. It took her two years to raise the necessary money, much of which she finally collected at small meetings, parlor gatherings, and sewing circles.

In November, 1837, Mount Holyoke received its first students. The three-year course of study compared well with the academic curricula of the better men's colleges. But Mary Lyon insisted that academic excellence must be combined with a practical orientation. "We must consider the good of the whole. . . . The young lady needs to feel herself the member of a large community, where the interests of others are to be sought equally with her own."

Prior to the opening of Mount Holyoke, women had been admitted only to Oberlin College. Mount Holyoke set the example for the formation of separate educational institutions for women. The opening of Vassar in 1865 was followed in the next twenty-five years by the establishment of several well-endowed women's colleges, equal to the best schools available to men. Western land grant colleges opened their doors from the beginning to men and women. By the late nineteenth century an educated elite of women was clamoring for acceptance in all the professions without discrimination.

Women in the Professions

The exclusion of women from all the major professions was due to the professionalization of medicine, the sciences, and the law in the early decades of the nineteenth century. Once academic training had become established as a prerequisite for professional standing, women, as long as they were excluded from such training, were virtually shut out.

Medicine. This was particularly true in the medical profession where very few women practitioners could be found between the American Revolution and the 1850's. The few still practicing were regarded as quacks. Dr. Harriot Hunt, who had been in practice in Boston since 1835, having acquired her train-

45

ing through private apprenticeship with a British practitioner, was denied admission to Harvard Medical School in 1847 and again in 1850.

The first woman formally admitted to medical school was Elizabeth Blackwell, who in 1849 graduated at the head of her class from Geneva College. Even so, she encountered insurmountable prejudices in trying to set up a practice. In 1857 she had to found her own institution, the New York Infirmary for Women, to enable her and several other women doctors to earn a precarious living. The Philadelphia Female Medical College, founded in 1853, was the first institution of its kind. It took years of difficult struggle for its graduates to be accorded professional recognition and the chance to earn a living as doctors.

The position of midwives similarly deteriorated in the early nineteenth century. Women had held a virtual monopoly of this profession in colonial America, but by the 1840's they were virtually excluded from the practice of midwifery on the eastern seaboard. Their place was taken by obstetrically trained male physicians. Such midwives as were still practicing served mainly the poor. It is interesting to note that concepts of "propriety" shifted with the prevalent practice. In seventeenth-century Maine, the attempt of a man to act as a midwife had been considered outrageous and had subjected him to a lawsuit and a fine; in mid-nineteenth-century America, the suggestion that women should train as midwives and physicians was considered equally outrageous and improper.

Law and Business.   Professionalization similar to that of medicine occurred in the field of law. Before 1750, when lawsuits were commonly brought to the courts by the plaintiffs themselves or by deputies without specialized legal training, women as well as men could and did act as "attorneys-in-fact." When the law became a paid profession and trained lawyers took over litigation, women disappeared from the court scene for over a century.

A similar process of shrinking opportunities for women occurred in business and in the retail trades. There were fewer female storekeepers and business women in the 1830's than

46

there had been in colonial days. There was also a noticeable shift in the kind of merchandise handled by them. Where previously women could be found running almost every kind of retail shop, after 1830 they were mostly found in businesses that served women only.

The only fields in which professionalization did not result in the elimination of women were nursing and teaching. Both were characterized by a severe shortage of labor and bore the stigmas of low skill, low status, and low pay. Generally, nursing was regarded simply as an extension of the unpaid services performed by the housewife.

Society no longer approved of women working outside the home. To do so entailed a distinct loss of status. In fact, by the mid-nineteenth century respectable women in need of employment had only a very few occupational choices, all of them badly paid. Middle-class spinsters and widows, unless they wished to depend on their male relatives, were in a serious financial plight.

Arts and Science.   There are always exceptional individuals who are capable of surmounting the restrictions and constraints of their time. A few such women, at great personal sacrifice, succeeded in pioneering in new careers. Harriet Hosmer made her way as an artist. Maria Mitchell, the daughter of a Nantucket astronomer and trained by him, had a remarkable career in science. At the age of twenty-eight she discovered a comet and won international acclaim and recognition. In 1848 she became the first woman to be elected to the newly formed Academy of Arts and Sciences. She was a strong advocate of advanced education for women and later became a professor at Vassar College, as well as serving as president of the Association for the Advancement of Women.

Mary Gove Nichols and Paulina Wright Davis, who gave lectures to women on anatomy and physiology, were not as fortunate. Lacking access to academic training, they never progressed beyond amateur standing in their educational work. But they laid the groundwork for an interest in scientific education among women and, by their organizational and educational efforts, spurred scientific interest among them.

Margaret Fuller (1810–1850).   One of the most brilliant women of this period was Margaret Fuller. Educated by an exacting father who wished to prove her superior to any boy, she mastered the literary classics of six languages and was a child prodigy. Yet when her father died she was as badly prepared for shouldering the burden of supporting herself, her mother, and four younger children as any graduate of a female academy.

Her keen mind, astonishing erudition, and conversational skill soon gave her a place of leadership among Boston Transcendentalists (members of a literary and philosophical movement stressing the insights derived from instincts and emotions rather than from reason, and exalting man's conscience and closeness to nature). She was for many years the friend of men like Emerson, Bronson Alcott, and William Ellery Channing. She taught for a period in Alcott's experimental school, but soon perceived a more urgent need for educating women.

In 1839 she inaugurated what became known as Margaret Fuller's "Conversations," a group of lectures and discussions held in a bookshop in Boston. Her audiences were the bluestocking intellectuals of Boston. Her views found wider circulation through her contributions to and later co-editorship (with Emerson) of the *Dial,* a Transcendentalist literary journal. Here Margaret Fuller set the highest standards for literary criticism and proved, if nothing else, that certain gifted women could hold their own with men in the realm of ideas. In 1845 she joined the staff of the New York *Tribune,* published by Horace Greeley, as its first female reporter.

Margaret Fuller's activities as lecturer, critic and reporter made her a pioneer among women. Her contributions to women's rights will be discussed elsewhere. Her career ended tragically when, after a brief and passionately happy marriage to an Italian, she was drowned in a shipwreck with her husband and baby on her return from Italy.

Those who wished to prove the innate inferiority of women usually cited the absence of "great minds" among them. But great minds do not arise in a vacuum. The situation of nineteenth-century women in America is a good illustration of what happens to a group which for several generations is denied access to education. Women who were little more than literate and who were fettered by a low estimate of their intellectual potential could not be expected to become outstanding philosophers, writers, or scientists. It was left to the exceptional woman to make her own escape from ignorance. However, she could not do this without the help and support of some man, be it father, brother, or husband. Even a cursory survey of the biographies of most of the outstanding nineteenth-century women reveals that each of them had such a "supporting man" in her life. His role was generally to provide her with sufficient education and encouragement to enable her to strive for more ambitious goals.

Even so, the ambitious woman had to sacrifice the approval of her contemporaries and often make her way against great hostility, opposition and abuse. Although most of the outstanding women of the century were married, many of them married late, and a goodly number of them chose careers over marriage. This, it must be stressed, was a choice necessary in the nineteenth century because of the universal disapproval women met when stepping out of "their proper sphere"—the home. This had not been true in colonial America and is, of course, not true today. But the prejudices and restrictive ideas about woman's place undoubtedly hampered the unfolding of many female talents.

Women in Industry

The broad sweep of industrialization encompassed women from its inception. In Europe, the labor power of the early factories had consisted of displaced farmers. In America, men could always make a living at farming, and were not available or willing to enter the factories. From its beginnings, therefore, American industrialization depended on the labor of women and children.

As early as 1791, in his "Report on Manufactures," Alexander Hamilton had urged the employment of women and children, both for their own sake and for the benefit of society: "Women and children are rendered more useful, and the latter more early useful, by manufacturing establishments than they would otherwise be."

In 1816 a congressional committee reported that, of 100,000 industrial workers yearly producing $24,300,000 worth of goods, nearly two out of three were women and girls. Advocates of industrialization sang the praises of the working girl and advanced many arguments in favor of her employment. Typical of these is the statement by Mathew Carey in 1822, who commented favorably on the employment of young females, "who, but for this factory would have been without employment and spend their time perniciously—a burden to their parents and society—trained up to vicious courses—but thus happily preserved from idleness and its attendant vices and crimes. . . ."

Whether out of need or because factory work seemed more attractive than the unceasing drudgery on the farm, women flocked into the mills. In 1822 a report based on the fourth national census found women employed in over a hundred industrial occupations, chief among these the manufacture of textiles, hats, shoes, and paper. Women were also engaged in such unlikely trades as the manufacture of salt and pig iron.

The Lowell Girls.   In the early decades of the nineteenth century work in the New England textile industry showed few of the undesirable features characteristic of British industrialization. Women's wages, even though lower than those of men doing similar work, were adequate to live on in the company towns. In the model town of Lowell, Massachusetts, the employers set up boardinghouses, each run by a matron who supervised the morals as well as the comfort of the girls. If the girls had time and strength left after their twelve-and-a-half to fourteen-hour work day, they were encouraged to join organizations providing religious and moral uplift. The company boasted that its employees benefited so greatly by the system that a good number of them quit work after five to seven years, married, went west, and became teachers. The publication of a journal by the working girls, *The Lowell Offering,* which carried

Women workers lead shoemakers' strike in Lynn, Massachusetts, in 1860 saccharine poetry and romantic stories in no way distinguishable from those of the ladies' magazines, was further proof of the paternalistic regime in the mills.

But these supposedly idyllic conditions were soon exposed before the public by the workers themselves. One hundred and two mill girls joined a strike of men operatives in Pawtucket, Rhode Island, in 1824, which marked the beginning of organization among factory women. In 1834 the workers "turned-out" in Lowell at a signal given by a young girl who tossed her bonnet in the air. Wage cuts, demands for faster production, and the length of the working day were the main grievances. The girls also complained of overcrowded housing, exorbitant boardinghouse fees, and an employer blacklist against all workers who dared complain. The workers expressed these grievances by organizing a well-led union of mill girls. The Lowell Female Labor Reform Association, which lasted only two years (1845–1846), was led by Sarah Bagley, who can lay claim to being the first woman trade union leader in this country. The fledgling trade unionists published their own newspaper and

organized a petition campaign to the Massachusetts state legislature asking for a ten-hour day law. The resulting investigation by the legislature was the first of its kind in the United States.

But it was too early for unionization and labor reform legislation to succeed. Increasing mechanization changed factory conditions, and semi-skilled labor soon gave way to unskilled labor. With the start of large-scale Irish immigration in the 1840's, the relatively skilled and educated New England farmers' daughters came into competition with unskilled and desperately needy immigrant women who had no choice but to work at the barest subsistence wages. Within a decade immigrant workers and the poorest of native workers replaced farm girls in the mills and marked these factory occupations as the lowest in pay and status. Women remained untrained, casual labor, and soon were relegated by custom to the lowest paid jobs. Long hours, overwork, and poor working conditions came to characterize women's work in industry for almost a century.

Home Industry. The development of factory work was paralleled by the spread of home industry. The needle trades and fashion industry in particular depended entirely on the labor of needy women, who were heavily exploited. Barred by lack of skill and training opportunities from more remunerative occupations, these women were forced to work at pitiful piecework rates in the home. Their ability to survive at all frequently depended on their making use of the unpaid subsidiary labor of their children. "It requires great expertness and unceasing industry from sunrise to ten and eleven at night, constant employment, which very few of them have . . . to earn a dollar and a half per week," wrote a contemporary in 1829, describing the work of seamstresses in Philadelphia. He added that many of these seamstresses were unable to survive the winter, even though fully occupied, without some form of charitable relief.

Whether working at piecework or factory rates, women earned a third to a fourth of men's wages. "A woman who goes out to wash," observed Sarah Grimké in 1837, "works as hard in proportion as a wood sawyer or a coal heaver, but she is not generally able to make more than half as much for a day's work." Seamstresses averaged $1.25 per week or less, and mothers of young children needing care might average only $36.40 annually. Early efforts to improve the plight of these home workers by organizing them were unsuccessful. Domestic industry remained the most underpaid of all occupations.

A further result of industrialization was an increasing division among women by class. The mill girls, pieceworkers, and factory hands were separated by a great gulf from the middle-class and wealthier housewives and ladies. Magazine and novel writers and even reformers largely ignored women workers, showing only sporadic concern with their plight. Yet their economic contribution to American abundance was considerable. While working women did not yet share in the wealth they created, promises of political and economic democracy gave them hope that their children would. While this hope was long deferred, the movement of women into industrial employment was an important step forward in advancing their opportunities.

CHAPTER FIVE

The West
and the South

After 1815 it is almost impossible to make any generalization about American women; their situation depended on the region they lived in. The eastern seaboard was the most advanced. In the frontier regions of the West, conditions of life during the nineteenth century resembled very closely those described for colonial women.

Frontier Life

As the frontier moved westward throughout the nineteenth century, women moved with it. They were in the exploring parties opening Oregon and Washington to white settlement. They were on the California and Oregon trails and wherever homesteaders followed the trappers and hunters to settle in the wide open plains. The journey westward was enormously difficult. Not infrequently the wagons were so heavily loaded there was no room for passengers; many a woman had to walk the entire distance of the journey carrying a baby and leading her other children by the hand. One traveler described a group of women and children in the Great Plains in 1852:

> An open, bleak prairie, the cold wind howling overhead, bearing with it the mournful tones of that deserted woman; a new made grave, a woman and three children sitting near by; a girl of fourteen summers walking round and round in a circle, wringing her hands and calling upon her dead parent; a boy of twelve sitting upon the waggon tongue, sobbing aloud; a strange man placing a rude head-board at the head of the grave.[6]

The weak and feeble could not survive the hardships of pioneering, and deaths were frequent. So were births, and women found themselves alone in meeting these terrifying experiences. Abigail Scott Duniway described her own pioneer life in a moving account:

> In the spring of 1852 my father decided to emigrate to Oregon. My invalid mother expostulated in vain; she and nine of us children were stowed away in ox-wagons, where for six months we made our home, cooking food and washing dishes around campfires, sleeping at night in the wagons, and crossing many streams upon wagon-beds, rigged as ferry-boats. When our weary line of march had reached the Black Hills of Wyoming my mother became a victim to the dreadful epidemic, cholera, that devastated the emigrant trains in that never-to-be-forgotten year, and after a few hours' illness her weary spirit was called to the skies. We made her a grave in the solitudes of the eternal hills, and again took up our line of march, "too sad to talk, too dumb to pray." But ten weeks after, our Willie, the baby, was buried in the sands of the Burnt River mountains.[7]

Her family settled in a small community in Oregon where Abigail Duniway became a schoolteacher, then married and lived the ordinary life of a frontier wife and mother. She bore

six children and had the not unusual experience of providing not only for her own household but for a raft of male boarders who brought a little income to the family:

> I, if not washing, scrubbing, churning or nursing the baby, was preparing their meals in our lean-to kitchen. To bear two children in two and a half years from my marriage day, to make thousands of pounds of butter every year for market, not including what was used in our free hotel at home; to sew and cook, and wash and iron; to bake and clean and stew and fry; to be, in short, a general pioneer drudge, with never a penny of my own, was not pleasant business for an erstwhile school teacher.[8]

After such experiences it is little wonder that Mrs. Duniway became the leading feminist of the Northwest. In her seventies, she had the satisfaction of writing the woman's suffrage proclamation for the state of Oregon.

While from 1820 on the sex ratio was even in the East, women remained scarce in the West. As the frontier moved further west, urbanization increased in the Midwest. In the decade before the Civil War, the development of Ohio and Illinois roughly paralleled that of the East at an earlier period. Even as late as the 1880's, women in the Far West suffered the hardships and enjoyed the advantages that had characterized the lives of eastern women one hundred years earlier.

The South

In the mountainous regions of the South, where yeoman farming and free labor prevailed, conditions were similar to those on the western frontier. But in the plantation South economic and social conditions developed in an unbroken pattern from colonial days to the Civil War, so sharply differentiating the South from the rest of the country that we refer to it as a separate and distinct culture.

57

Plantation Mistresses.　　　The wives and daughters of planters performed an important function on the slave plantation. While they did no manual labor and seldom took personal care of their own children, they supervised and were responsible for the running of the household in every last detail. A slave plantation was an independent economic unit, frequently almost wholly self-supporting. As many as 150 men, women, and children were fed, clothed, and housed entirely under the jurisdiction of the master and mistress.

While the plantation mistress had little or no dealings with the field slaves in their work, she usually would minister to them in sickness and supervise their housing, health, and religious instruction, if any. The coarse Negro cloth and simple clothing was made under her direction, the fruits of farm and field were processed under her instruction. The personal servants in attendance to each of her children were trained by her, and she decided on reward and punishment for them.

In addition to these domestic responsibilities, the plantation mistress also had to play the role of the wife of a leading citizen in the county. This implied much visiting, entertaining, and charitable and church work. Plantation families usually hired tutors for the instruction of their sons and daughters. The sons would continue their higher education in the North and in England, while the daughters proceeded to early marriages.

The wives of the small class of plantation overseers, professional men, and middle-class townsmen attempted in every way to ape the standards of behavior of the plantation ladies.

There was a much sharper division between the activities of men and women in slave society than there was among the landed gentry of the North. Planters occupied a great part of their time with hunting, gambling, supervision of their far-flung business interests, and other purely male pursuits. The planter's wives spent a great deal of time in the company of slaves and children, or of each other.

But the southern white woman could glory in receiving the most chivalrous treatment in the nation. If the North practiced a cult of the "lady," the South put "white womanhood" on a pedestal. "The defense of white womanhood" became the battle cry for all those who defended slavery against its critics. The British writer Harriet Martineau criticized this concept of chivalry rather sharply:

> While woman's intellect is confined, her morals crushed, her health ruined, her weakness encouraged, and her strength punished, she is told that her lot is cast in the paradise of women: and there is no country in the world where there is so much boasting of the "chivalrous" treatment she enjoys. . . . Her husband's hair stands on end at the idea of her working, and he toils to indulge her with money. . . . In short, indulgence is given her as a substitute for justice.
>
> Her case differs from that of the slave, as to the principle, just so far as this; that the indulgence is large and universal, instead of petty and capricious.[9]

The South lagged behind the rest of the nation in education and in the development of transportation and industry. Plantation society resisted change and innovation and was essentially conservative. At a time when humanitarian reformers in the North and West were agitating for social change, Southerners were preoccupied with defending their slavery system and keeping out men and ideas that seemed to threaten it.

Inevitably, women shared in the general culture. Southern women therefore did not participate in the reform activities of the mid-century, nor did they raise demands of their own. The only outstanding female reformers from their ranks, the Grimké sisters from South Carolina, were forced into exile by the ostracism of their community. The Ante-Bellum South protected its women from the uncertainties and complexities of choices. In no other part of the United States was domesticity so firmly enshrined; nowhere else was the position of women as circumscribed.

Slave Women.   The lives of black women were equally rigidly defined. Of all American women, black women were the most degraded, most exploited, most disadvantaged. The female slave, like the male, was legally a chattel, a human property that could be bought, sold, traded, mortgaged, and rented. Her value depended on age, health, and physical condition, in short on the amount of labor one could reasonably hope to extract from her. In addition, the slave woman was valued for her sex and childbearing ability. The highest market value was realized by the sale of females who had already borne one or two children. Such women were frequently advertised as "good breeders."

While generalizations about slavery falter on the fact that there were as many varieties of conditions as there were masters, all slaves were deprived of basic human and all civil rights. Their food, shelter, working conditions, clothing, health care, and punishment were entirely at the discretion of their masters. Their testimony against a white person was not recognized in any court. They were restricted by law to their place of employment, from which they were not permitted to move without a pass signed by their master. While slave law restrained the master from inflicting excessively cruel punishment on his slaves, the definition of what constituted "excessively cruel" punishment was rather vague. A master could not be tried even for killing his slave, if he could offer some justification for the deed. In case of resistance, flight or rebellion, a slow and painful death was the common punishment.

The excessive severity of the slave law was frequently tempered in practice, and some slaves were treated with a fair amount of decency. But, slavery was above all a labor system; as such it depended on extracting the maximum amount of unpaid labor from totally dependent and legally unprotected slaves, and terror and fear were essential ingredients for the success of such a system.

There were no legal and few practical distinctions between the treatment of male and female slaves. Women, as well as men, were expected to work from sun-up to sundown. Customarily, pregnant field slaves carried a lighter work load for a few months and did not work for three or four weeks after their confinement. But there is much evidence that, even on the best run plantations, provisions for the health needs of female slaves were minimal.

Frances Kemble, the British actress who married an American plantation owner, Pierce Butler, and spent several unhappy months on his Georgia plantation, has left a touching account of the casual abuse of female slaves. She listened to innumerable appeals from the slave women, whose main request was that they be allowed four weeks' instead of only three weeks' respite from field work after their confinement. (Frances Kemble never succeeded in getting this favor for the slaves despite her entreaties to her husband.) These were one day's petitioners, as recorded in her diary:

> Fanny has had six children; all dead but one. . . .
> Sophy . . . came to beg for some old linen. She is suffering fearfully; she has had ten children; five of them are dead.
> Sally . . . has had two miscarriages and three children born, one of whom is dead. She came complaining of incessant pain and weakness in her back.
> Sarah . . . She had had four miscarriages, had brought seven children into the world, five of whom were dead, and was again with child. She complained of dreadful pains in the back, and an internal tumor which swells with the exertion of working in the fields; probably, I think, she is ruptured. . . .
> Molly . . . Hers was the best account I have yet received; she had had nine children, and six of them were still alive. . . .
> There was hardly one of these . . . who might not have been a candidate for a bed in a hospital, and they had come to me after working all day in the fields.[10]

One woman had a particularly dismal story to tell:

> She had had sixteen children, fourteen of whom were dead; she had had four miscarriages: one had been caused with falling down with a very heavy burden on her head, and one from having her arms strained up to be lashed. . . . She said their hands were first tied together . . . and they were then drawn up to a tree or post, and then their

clothes rolled round their waist, and a man with a cowhide stands and stripes them. I give you the woman's words. She did not speak of this as of anything strange, unusual or especially horrid and abominable; and when I said: "Did they do that to you when you were with child?" She simply replied: "Yes, missis." and to all this I listen—I an Englishwoman, the wife of the man who owns these wretches, and I cannot say: "That thing shall not be done again. ..." I ... remained choking with indignation and grief long after they had all left me to my most bitter thoughts.[11]

Frances Kemble's account is unique only because she bothered to listen to the complaints of women and gave vent to her indignation over what she heard and saw. Other eyewitnesses to plantation slavery corroborated her observations including the evidence of the sexual exploitation of slave women.

The female slave had no defense against the sexual advances of any white man, and neither marriage nor motherhood protected her from the abuse of her owner and the overseer. Since by slave law the child followed the legal condition of his mother, any offspring of miscegenation became the owner's property and slave.

Another plantation mistress and a staunch defender of the Confederacy remarked on prevailing conditions in the privacy of her diary:

God forgive us, but ours is a monstrous system. ... Like the patriarchs of old, our men live all in one house with their wives and their concubines; and the mulattoes one sees in every family partly resemble the white children. Any lady is ready to tell you who is the father of all the mulatto children in everybody's household but her own. Those, she seems to think, drop from the clouds.[12]

It was to the advantage of the master to have his female slaves bear as many children as possible and to sell those children if he could not find enough useful work for them to do.

The separation of children from their mothers, a practice which was considered disreputable among slaveholders, was nevertheless quite widespread. It occurred most frequently in periods of economic stress or as the result of the death of a master and the splitting up of his inheritance among children and creditors.

In slave society, just as in the surrounding white culture, there were hierarchies of status and privilege. Lowest on the scale were the field hands, especially those on the sugar and rice plantations of the deep South. The large group comprised of slaves owned by small farmers were somewhat better off, since they worked beside their masters and were often treated with more humanity than the slaves laboring in gangs. Unskilled house servants were next in rank, with skilled artisans enjoying the best position. A small, but significant group of free Negroes had a precarious existence in the cities of the North and South. Among them, artisans and small businessmen in the service trades were the elite.

For slave women only the domestic skills offered any chance of improving their condition. Sewing, fine starching, ironing, cooking, and nursing were the most valued skills. The black "Mammy," celebrated in southern myth and literature, was often second only to her mistress in authority and prestige. It must be remembered, however, that her position of authority, such as it was, derived from her being a substitute mother to the owner's children, which of necessity demanded that she neglect her own.

The Free Black Woman.   The free black woman had few marketable skills, except sewing and nursing. The vast majority had to work in service occupations or as washerwomen. Many of these managed by sheer drudgery at the most menial tasks to earn enough money to purchase the freedom of their children. In the cities of the North, the economic and social position of free Negroes was only slightly better than in the South.

The lack of education for black children was a universal grievance, for no state admitted black children to its public schools. The black communities struggled to educate their children by setting up their own schools and training their own teachers. One of the unsung heroines of this struggle was Catherine Ferguson, born a slave, who was later permitted by her master to purchase her own freedom. It is not known where she acquired what education she may have had, but in 1793 she took forty-eight children, twenty of whom were white, out of an almshouse and opened "Katy Ferguson's School for the Poor" in New York City.

Sarah Douglass, a black Quaker woman from Philadelphia, also made a notable contribution to raising the educational level of her people. Having received a good education in Quaker schools, Miss Douglass began teaching in a school for black children run by Quaker ladies. After a few years she took over the running of the school on her own and for many years pioneered in raising educational standards. Finally, she had the distinction of being the first black woman to be appointed as a public school teacher in Philadelphia.

Ironically, black women enjoyed an advantage over white women—their status within their own group was higher. Many of the African societies from which slaves came were agricultural societies in which women were in charge of the planting and were therefore accorded a position of considerable esteem. In many of these societies descent was reckoned, and property transmitted, through the female line. Some African cultures allowed women a considerable voice in tribal councils. Women were also believed to have magical powers and to know the secrets of healing herbs and roots.

There has been some disagreement among historians, sociologists, and anthropologists as to how much of this African heritage was carried to the New World. Even if one assumes that most of it was destroyed by the brutal voyage across the Atlantic and by life on the plantations, there are indications that it survived as a tradition.

The conditions of American slavery created a distorted family life, in which the black man was deprived of the ability to support, protect, and defend his family. Any sign of resistance to the master was severely punished and, if this failed to break the spirit of the slave, he was sold. Such punishment was more frequently meted out to male slaves than to women. Slave families were ruthlessly separated when it was to the economic advantage of the master, but mother and child were generally kept together, at least for the early years of a child's life. This made the slave mother the only stable element in the slave family. The authority of the mother in the slave cabin was undisputed.

In their role as house servants, slave women were in close contact with the mistress, her children and, at times, the master. Many a black servant used this intimate contact to win some small advantage for herself or her children. Under slavery, not only was the black male deprived of authority over his family, but the role of the father was usurped by the white master. Since it was he who held absolute power over the fate of women and children, it was natural that they should turn to him rather than to the powerless black men for protection.

It is remarkable that, despite these enormous pressures, black families struggled to establish and maintain stability. During Reconstruction and after, black men assumed responsibility as heads of families whenever they could find work to support their families. But poverty and racial discrimination placed an added burden on black women, even in modern America. They could find work more readily than did their men because they were not viewed with as much suspicion and hostility by whites. This work was generally housework or menial labor in factories. Because of racial discrimination against black men, black married women, in proportionally greater numbers than their white counterparts, had to stay in the labor force. Many of them were the sole support of their families. These factors, plus the tendency of modern welfare legislation to encourage the abandonment of poor families by the father in order to make the family eligible for aid, account for the abnormally large number of black families headed by women. But despite all obstacles most black families (three out of four, according to the 1960 census) are headed by a father.

Resistance to Oppression

Under slavery, few historical records were kept of individual slaves. Once in a while a spectacularly dramatic story would find its way into the columns of newspapers. One such story was that of Margaret Garner, a slave who had escaped to Cincinnati with her husband and four children, only to be recaptured. While her husband was led away, she killed her three-year-old girl, and was only prevented from killing the other children by being overpowered. When her captors transported her down the Ohio River back to slavery, she allowed her baby to fall overboard "by accident." The boat was later shipwrecked and Margaret Garner, eluding her captors and would-be rescuers, was finally able to find freedom in death.

Apart from individual desperate instances such as this of resistance to slavery, there were a few black women whose unbreakable spirit and lifelong dedication to the fight against oppression brought them enduring fame.

Harriet Tubman (c. 1820–1913).   Born a slave in Maryland, Harriet Tubman is famous for being the most daring "conductor" on the Underground Railroad. After her master's death, she feared that she would be sold and decided to escape. Her husband, a freedman, refused to join her, so she made her way to freedom without him. She returned repeatedly to her old plantation until she had rescued her entire family.

Due to an old head injury, incurred while aiding the escape of a slave, she was seriously handicapped by fainting spells that came upon her without warning. But with tremendous courage, tenacity, and practical wisdom she managed to overcome all obstacles in her effort to bring slaves north to freedom. She always carried a pistol with her. When a slave faltered under the hardships of the trip and proposed to return to slavery or begged to be left behind, she would draw her pistol on him and declare, "You go on or die." Nobody ever doubted that she would make good her threat. When carrying infants she would drug them into deep sleep and conceal them in a sack. The slaves called her "Moses" and credited her with supernatural powers. Over the years, the slaveholders offered a total of $40,-000 in rewards for her capture. During a ten-year period Harriet Tubman made nineteen trips into slave territory and rescued over three hundred slaves. It was her pride that she never lost a single "passenger."

Harriet Tubman performed invaluable services as a scout and nurse during the Civil War and in old age organized and supported a home for aged freedmen.

Sojourner Truth (c. 1797–1893).   Another remarkable slave woman was Isabella Baumfree, known by her chosen name, "Sojourner Truth." Born a slave in the last years of the eighteenth century in Ulster County, New York, she saw all her twelve brothers and sisters sold off by her Dutch master. After his death, Belle was sold together with a herd of sheep to John Neely, who beat her for not understanding his English commands. Sold twice before the age of fourteen and raped by her master, Belle was then forcibly married to an older slave.

By 1817, when New York abolished slavery for adults, she had borne five children, of whom four were alive. She was freed with her youngest child, but learned that her boy, Peter, was still enslaved, although his owner had promised him his freedom. Determined to save him, Belle took the daring step of suing for his freedom in the state court, and won the case. She supported herself and her children as a domestic worker in New York City, joined a utopian religious colony and engaged in another spectacular law suit during which she sued a white man for slander and won complete vindication.

Her increasingly powerful, mystical visions convinced her that she must become an itinerant preacher. She adopted the name "Sojourner Truth" and began preaching for freedom all over the North. In 1851 the tall, thin woman appeared at a Woman's Rights Convention in Akron, Ohio, and asked to address the audience. The previous speaker, a clergyman, had ridiculed the weakness of women and argued that they could not be entrusted with equal rights. She answered him in these words:

> The man over there says women need to be helped in carriages and lifted over ditches, and to have the best place everywhere. Nobody ever helps me into carriages or over puddles, or gives me the best place—and ain't I a woman? Look at my arm! I have ploughed and planted and gathered into barns, and no man could head me—and ain't I a

woman? I could work as much and eat as much as a man —when I could get it—and bear the lash as well! And ain't I a woman? I have borne thirteen children, and seen most of 'em sold into slavery, and when I cried out with my mother's grief, none but Jesus heard me—and ain't I a woman?[13]

Sojourner Truth's pithy arguments and dignified personality had tremendous impact on her audiences. She was fearless and had an overpowering self-confidence, which was based on her belief that God talked to her. This faith made her impervious to insults and attack. Once, after she had debated a bigoted lawyer, the man sneered contemptuously, "You think your talk does any good, old woman? Why, I don't care any more for it than for a fleabite." "Maybe not," Sojourner replied calmly. "But the Lord willing, I'll keep you scratching."

After the Civil War she was appointed by the Freedmen's Bureau to train black women for employment. Well over eighty, she made it her business to board the Jim Crow Washington streetcars, seat herself in the white compartment, and force the conductors to throw her off, protesting. Even though she could not single-handedly break this discriminatory law, she saw to it that every such incident became a lesson in cruelty and inhumanity which the white onlookers would not soon forget.

Sojourner Truth, whose life was an unceasing struggle against race prejudice, proved that extraordinary strength could overcome brutality, illiteracy, bitter poverty, and constant discrimination. The wizened old woman with her symbolic name and her shrewd folk wit was the voice of tens of thousands of anonymous suffering black women.

The Contributions of Black Women. There are no figures available on the productivity of slave labor. We do know, however, that cotton was the major export staple of the United States before the Civil War, and that cotton profits were the foundation of the wealth of southern states and northern industry. Unpaid slave labor helped create this wealth. A good half of the slave labor force were women. Thus, it can readily

68

be seen that the contribution of black women to the pre-Civil War economy was sizeable.

The cultural contribution black women made as house servants and nurses and their subtle impact on the impressionable minds of white children also cannot be fully assessed. But neither should they be ignored. Sentimentalized and stereotyped as the "Mammy" of fiction, the black woman has never yet received her due. Her accomplishment in bearing her hard lot without rancor and caring for the master's offspring with warmth and affection, and in providing her own family with whatever stability was possible, was truly remarkable. The black woman is the forgotten heroine of our history.

CHAPTER SIX

Women Organize
for Reform and Welfare

The earliest women's organizations grew out of church work. Usually the women met weekly in sewing circles to make garments, quilts, or other saleable items. In the so-called "cent societies" members also contributed one cent a week as dues. The funds raised were donated to the upkeep of the church or to the training of worthy young men for the ministry. The ladies often combined the useful with the cultural by reading and discussing books as they sewed. The earliest literary societies grew out of these sewing circles. In the late 1820's women began to support a variety of organizations—Bible and missionary societies, temperance groups, and "Magdalen Societies" for the salvation of "fallen women." However, the leadership of all these reform organizations remained in the hands of men, most of them ministers.

Social Welfare

Quaker women pioneered in organizing orphan asylums, free schools for the poor or for black children, and prison aid societies. Other religious denominations did not lag far behind. A "Society for the Relief of poor Widows and small Children," formed in New York City by fifteen ladies in 1797, supported 202 widows and 500 children by 1816, collecting and dispensing over $3500 a year for charity. These ladies organized social work in a systematic and businesslike manner, with a board of manageresses supervising home visitors, keeping records on their charges, and disbursing funds in line with carefully worked out directives. Their approach was to help only the "worthy poor," and immediately to cut off relief to any woman tainted with immoral conduct, drunkenness, or lack of piety. They also set up and managed a home for orphans and a workshop for needy mothers. Similar relief work was organized in other cities.

Dorothea Dix (1802–1889).   That it was possible for one outraged woman to have a tremendous impact on society even without the support of an organization was proven by a frail, thirty-nine-year-old Boston spinster named Dorothea Dix. In 1841, in ill health and no longer able to pursue her avocation as a schoolteacher, Dorothea Dix volunteered to lead the Sunday school class in the Cambridge jail. Thus was launched one of the most remarkable careers in American reform history.

In the Cambridge jail, Dorothea Dix discovered what she could have found in any jail in the United States at that time —filthy conditions, no heat, and insane people lodged with criminals because there was no other place to keep them. Outraged, she set out to visit every jail in New England and to record the results of her investigation. These she presented a few years later to the legislature of Massachusetts. It was the first report of its kind, and a remarkable document:

> I shall be obliged to speak with great plainness, and to reveal many things revolting to the taste, and from which my woman's nature shrinks with peculiar sensitiveness. But truth is the highest consideration. *I tell what I have seen* —painful and shocking as the details often are. . . .
>
> I come as the advocate of helpless, forgotten, insane and idiotic men and women; of beings, sunk to a condition from which the most unconcerned would start with real

horror; of beings wretched in our Prisons, and more wretched in our alms-houses. . . . Chained, naked, beaten with rods and lashed into obedience. . . .

Concord. A woman from the hospital in a cage in the alms-house. In the jail several, decently cared for in general, but not properly placed in a prison. Violent, noisy, unmanageable most of the time. . . .

Medford. One idiotic subject chained, and one in a close stall for 17 years. . . .

The use of cages all but universal; hardly a town but can refer to some not distant period of using them; chains are less common; negligences frequent; wilful abuse less frequent than sufferings proceeding from ignorance, or want of consideration. . . .[14]

With a vision unusual for her day, Dorothea Dix discussed what improved conditions could mean, not only for the wretched people affected, but for the entire community:

Hospitals are the only place where insane persons can be properly controlled. . . . With proper care and attention, lunatics may not only be made comfortable but in many instances restored again to society with sound minds. . . . Gentlemen, I commit to you this sacred cause.[15]

Shock, outrage and ridicule greeted her exposé, but upon investigation every one of her charges was documented. The bills she had requested passed the Massachusetts legislature. Dorothea Dix had found her mission. Between 1844 and 1854 she traveled more than 30,000 miles to reform the penal system and the care of the mentally ill in the United States and ultimately in Europe. Her spirit is best expressed in her own words: "They say nothing can be done here. I reply, I know no such word in the vocabulary I adopt."

She visited eighteen state penitentiaries, three hundred jails and over five hundred almshouses. She published a detailed report of her findings and urged the remodelling of all county jails, the separation of first offenders from hardened criminals, education for prisoners, and separate institutions for women.

73

Dorothea Dix

In 1848 Dorothea Dix approached Congress with a "Memorial . . . praying a grant of land for the relief and support of the indigent insane in the United States." She offered a documented survey of existing conditions and a detailed program for reform. She urged Congress to consider the insane "wards of the nation" and to finance their care with a federal land grant of five million acres. She lobbied for three years on behalf of her program, establishing an office in the Library of Congress from which she bombarded Congress with charges, documents, and arguments. She extended her recommendations to include the care of the blind, deaf, and dumb. Although the bill was finally passed in 1854, it was vetoed by President Pierce, who regarded it as an invasion of states' rights.

In 1861 Dorothea Dix was appointed Superintendent of Nurses, the first such office instituted in United States history. After her war services, she resumed her activities on behalf of the handicapped and ill with undiminished vigor until her death in 1887.

Before Dorothea Dix began her campaign, there existed thirteen institutions for the care of the insane in the United States. In 1880, largely thanks to her efforts, there were 123 such institutions. She had personally founded, designed, and planned thirty-five of these. Fifteen training schools for the feeble-minded, nursing schools, the permanent Army Nurses Corps, and literally hundreds of prisons, poorhouses, and county jails which had adopted her reforms were a monument to her spirit. Her accomplishment is unequalled in the history of reform.

Most women had neither the strength nor the fanatic devotion of Dorothea Dix; they needed to work with others to achieve their goals. Temperance and abolition were the two reforms of the pre-Civil War period that seemed to attract the most women.

Antislavery Women

In 1833, when delegates met in Philadelphia to form the American Anti-Slavery Society, three women attended the convention as observers. A few days later twenty women met to form the Philadelphia Female Anti-Slavery Society. From that time on, northern women played an important part in the movement for the abolition of slavery and for the integration of the Negro into American society. In the next decade they set up a great number of female antislavery societies. By the 1840's there were roughly as many men as women organized into these groups.

The women very early began to use petitions as a means of influencing public opinion and gaining adherents. "The right of petition is the only political right that women have," Angelina Grimké pointed out. Many others agreed; tens of thousands of petitions against slavery flooded Congress and the state legislatures, serving to arouse public opinion and stir up debate on this highly controversial subject. Antislavery women also organized fairs and bazaars to raise funds and pioneered in setting up youth groups to educate a new generation of antislavery workers.

Lucretia Mott (1793–1880).   The best in antislavery leadership was epitomized by Lucretia Mott. The mother of six children, she had the standing of a Quaker minister in her Philadelphia society and was experienced in public speaking. Her gentle, lady-like appearance concealed a razor-sharp mind and a stubborn determination. Mrs. Mott was known to stop mobs with the same firmness that she would use on an unruly child. She founded the Philadelphia Female Anti-Slavery Society and remained for over forty years its president and leading member. She was also instrumental in organizing the early Woman's Rights movement.

Lucretia Mott was a convincing speaker and frequently lectured to large audiences outside her Quaker circle, but her main impact was that of an organizer and pace-setter. One had only to look at the motherly, genteel Lucretia Mott and listen to her opinions and speeches to become convinced that it was possible for women to combine femininity with active participation in the political and social life of their time.

The antislavery women were as intrepid as their brothers and husbands when it came to meeting mobs or threats of violence. In fact, they developed what we know as nonviolent resistance to a fine art. A memorable occasion on which the technique was used was in Boston in 1835, when a furious mob of citizens surrounded a meeting of the Boston Female Anti-Slavery Society at which William Lloyd Garrison was featured as the speaker. Appeals to the mayor for protection proved fruitless. Instead, he informed the women that the presence of black women in their midst justifiably enraged the citizens and asked them to send their Negro members home. This the women refused to do and the chairman, Mrs. Chapman, replied, "If this is the last bulwark of freedom, we may as well die here as anywhere." The ladies continued their meeting for a time, but spirited Garrison away to another room. Then each white woman took a black sister by the hand, and they walked out through the mob in orderly procession, staring down their attackers with quiet dignity. Meanwhile, Garrison was dragged through the streets at the end of a rope and finally had to be lodged in the town jail for safekeeping. This Boston mob had the effect of winning important new adherents to the antislavery movement and made the courage of abolitionist women a legend.

The Grimké Sisters—Sarah M. Grimké (1792–1873) and Angelina E. Grimké Weld (1805–1879). The participation of women in political life was lifted to a new level during the winter and spring of 1837–1838, when the "woman question" was first raised as an issue confronting reformers. The crisis was precipitated by two most unlikely agents of social revolution, Sarah and Angelina Grimké, natives of South Carolina. The Grimké sisters were that greatest of rarities, southern abolitionists.

Daughters of the assistant chief justice of South Carolina, the Grimké sisters were raised in a typical plantation household. What they saw of slavery shocked them, and they attempted to convince others of the sinfulness of the system. Finally, realizing that they could not help to effect any changes while remaining in the South, the sisters chose exile in the North. They became Quakers and, much later, abolitionists. Angelina Grimké wrote a stirring antislavery appeal to southern women, which was publicly burned in Charleston. She was threatened with immediate imprisonment should she ever return. Before long both sisters had taken the decisive step of becoming "agents" and traveling lecturers of the American Anti-Slavery Society.

The sisters' spectacular lecture tour in New England attracted large audiences who came not only to hear what they had to say but to enjoy the unprecedented spectacle of women speaking in public. It was impossible to dismiss the pious, utterly respectable, and impeccably lady-like Grimké sisters as freaks and lunatics. In an effort to weaken their audience appeal, the Council of Congregationalist Churches issued a pastoral letter warning "against the dangers which at the present seem to threaten the female character with widespread and permanent injury." If a woman "assumed the place and tone of man as a public reformer," she would "fall in shame and dishonor into the dust."

While this blast did not have the desired effect on New England audiences, it did provoke a vigorous debate on the

woman question in abolitionist circles. In this debate the Grimké sisters performed one of their most notable services by refusing in any way to disassociate their abolitionism from their insistence that as women they had a perfect right to speak in public. "Woman must feel that she is the equal and is designed to be the fellow laborer of her brother," Sarah Grimké declared. "I ask no favors for my sex. . . . All I ask our brethren is, that they will take their feet from off our necks, and permit us to stand upright on that ground which God designed us to occupy."

The sisters ended their speaking tour with Angelina Grimké presenting an antislavery petition, signed by twenty thousand women, to the Massachusetts legislature. It was the first time any woman had ever testified before a legislative committee.

It took two more years before the full impact of these pioneering events was felt in reform circles. By then, the Grimké sisters' example had influenced a number of women who would later lead the movement for woman's rights.

When the woman question exploded in reform circles, it raised an issue American society had complacently ignored for five decades. If all men were created equal, why not woman? If woman was equal, why should she not do anything men might do—speak in public, vote, hold office, even lead organizations? Once these questions had been raised, it was only a very short step to the next one: Why should not women organize to help themselves and gain the rights denied them?

(left) Lucretia Mott
(right) Angelina Grimké Weld

CHAPTER SEVEN

Women Ask
for Their Rights

In the Jacksonian era the United States was alive with a ferment
of ideas. Demands were heard for all kinds of reforms, from free
public schooling for every child to schemes for reforming the
drunkard, freeing the slaves and abolishing war forever. Small
wonder that women, too, began to question the position to
which they had been relegated by tradition and habit.

The Struggle for Equality

In 1836, the first petition for a law granting married women the
right to own property reached the New York state legislature.
It carried the signatures of six women and had been written and
circulated by Ernestine Rose, a recent immigrant. Ernestine
Rose, a Rabbi's daughter from Poland, later became one of the
most dynamic platform speakers of her day on behalf of
woman's rights. She continued circulating petitions until the
New York legislature finally, in 1849, enacted a law safeguard-
ing married women's property. Soon Mississippi, Pennsylvania,

California, and Wisconsin enacted similar measures. This was a small, but important step forward in giving women legal equality.

During the same period the right of divorce was first openly advocated. The passage of laws restricting child labor and making education compulsory in several states during the 1840's tended to weaken the absolute authority of the father over his children. From there it was an easy step to questioning the absolute authority of a man over his wife.

This questioning was evident even in areas of minor importance. When Angelina Grimké married abolitionist leader Theodore Weld, they devised a marriage ceremony that avoided the customary pledge of obedience by the wife to the husband. Instead, the couple pledged to love and cherish one another, and before their wedding signed an agreement whereby Weld renounced all claims to his wife's property. When Robert Dale Owen married Jane Robinson in 1832, he declared that he wished to be "utterly divested, now and during the rest of my life, of any such rights, the barbarous relics of a feudal, despotic system." When Lucy Stone and Henry Blackwell were married in 1855, they drew up a printed "protest" containing similar ideas. But Lucy Stone went further and, as a token of her independence, retained her maiden name after marriage.

The Right to Representation. To the thousands of educated volunteer workers in various reform organizations, the constant discrimination they suffered as women had become increasingly obnoxious. In 1840 the abolitionist movement split over the "woman question" when a woman was elected to the National Committee of the American Anti-Slavery Society. The actual causes of the division were much more profound than the question of a woman holding office, but the issue provided a handy excuse for precipitating a split. Henceforth there were two branches of the organized abolitionist movement, one permitting women to vote and hold office, the other exclusively male.

The woman's rights issue became international somewhat later that year when the Garrisonian abolitionists sent a number of women to the World Anti-Slavery Convention in London.

After heated discussion, the credentials of the female delegates were refused and they were seated behind a curtain in the gallery. In protest, William Lloyd Garrison and several of his followers walked out and joined the ladies. Among those seated in the gallery were Lucretia Mott and the young wife of the abolitionist Henry Stanton, Elizabeth. The two women soon became friends and spent long hours discussing what might be done to break down the prejudice against women. The personality and intellect of the older woman left a profound impression on Elizabeth Cady Stanton. "When I first heard from the lips of Lucretia Mott that I had the same right to think for myself that Luther, Calvin, and John Knox had, and the same right to be guided by my own convictions . . . I felt at once a new-born sense of dignity and freedom." The two women decided that upon their return to the United States they would call together a convention of women to discuss their condition. But eight years passed before they could carry out their resolution.

Elizabeth Cady Stanton (1815–1902).   A pretty, fun-loving girl, Elizabeth Cady grew up with four sisters in the well-to-do household of conservative Judge Cady, in upstate New York. The only boy in the family had died as a youth, and nothing any of the girls did could ever make up to Judge Cady for the fact that he had no son. Elizabeth grew up keenly resentful of the inferiority attached to being a girl. As a child she sat in her father's office and heard many female clients tell their sad stories, asking for redress against abusive husbands. In each case Judge Cady told them there were no laws which could give them aid. Young Elizabeth was so incensed by this that she once seriously proposed cutting out all the "bad laws" from the books. Her father patiently explained that this was not the way to change laws, and lectured her on the process by which laws are made and amended. It was a lesson she never forgot.

She married Henry Stanton over the strong objections of her father, who resented the young man's radical, abolitionist views. After their return from the London convention, the young couple set up housekeeping in upstate New York. Henry Stanton became a lawyer, businessman, and politician, while his wife was fully occupied with running the household and taking care of her growing family of seven children. But she did not forget her idea of bringing women together to discuss their problems.

A "public meeting for protest and discussion" was finally decided upon by Mrs. Stanton and Lucretia Mott during a social visit. They and three other women drafted a call for such a meeting, but in their inexperience they did not trust themselves to find the proper words for defining their purpose. After some thought they hit upon the idea of using the Declaration of Independence as a model. They paraphrased the original, sentence by sentence:

> We hold these truths to be self-evident: that all men and women are created equal: that they are endowed by their Creator with certain inalienable rights: that among these are life, liberty and the pursuit of happiness. . . .
>
> The history of mankind is a history of repeated injuries and usurpations on the part of man toward woman, having in direct object the establishment of an absolute tyranny over her. To prove this, let facts be submitted to a candid world.[16]

The Seneca Falls Convention. On July 19, 1848, almost three hundred persons, including forty men, gathered in a small chapel at Seneca Falls, New York. Since none of the women felt equal to the task, the convention was presided over by James Mott. The speeches and resolutions stated a bold doctrine: woman was the equal of man and had the right and duty to participate "in all righteous causes," to speak in public, to teach, and to write. Women also demanded "equal participation with men in the various trades, professions and commerce."

The women who met at Seneca Falls were neither the most downtrodden nor the most abused of women. Yet each in her own way had experienced discrimination, a sense of frustration and a feeling of being relegated to second-class citizenship. One of them, nineteen-year-old Charlotte Woodward, the only one of those present who lived long enough to see women get the vote in the United States, has left a moving account of her reactions to the Seneca Falls convention. She, like so many others in the villages around Seneca Falls, had been employed as a homeworker, doing piecework for the glove factories. She recorded her feelings about her work:

> We women work secretly in the seclusion of our bed chambers because all society was built on the theory that men, not women, earned money and that men alone supported the family. . . . But I do not believe that there was any community in which the souls of some women were not beating their wings in rebellion. For my own obscure self I can say that every fibre of my being rebelled, although silently, all the hours that I sat and sewed gloves for a miserable pittance which, as it was earned, could never be mine. I wanted to work, but I wanted to choose my task and I wanted to collect my wages. That was my form of rebellion against the life into which I was born.[17]

The most controversial of all the resolutions was offered by Elizabeth Cady Stanton: "It is the sacred duty of the women of this country to secure to themselves their sacred right to the elective franchise." It almost failed to be adopted; only the vigorous supporting speech of the ex-slave and great black leader, Frederick Douglass, helped to secure enough votes to pass it by a small majority. For most women, suffrage was a remote concept, not nearly as pressing as most of their demands. But Judge Cady's daughter had not forgotten what it takes to change the nation's laws. She could not foresee that it would take seventy-two years of struggle to have her resolution translated into actuality. But, as she had expected, that meeting in the little upstate village set forces into motion which became, in time, a tremendous mass movement on behalf of woman's rights, not only in the United States but across the world.

The movement started modestly enough with annual state and national woman's rights conventions. While at the beginning these were nothing more than small local affairs subjected to bitter ridicule by the press and, at times, mob violence by an uncomprehending citizenry, they served an important function. As yet, only a very small minority of women were actively involved, and comparatively few were convinced of the justice of the demands being raised by the feminists. But the woman's rights conventions taught women to speak for themselves, to initiate broad mass campaigns, to engender public discussion and win male supporters, to make their voices heard in the legislative halls, and to stand up to the abuse of press and public.

After the Seneca Falls convention, talented individuals who wanted a chance for education and a wider sphere of activity than was offered by the home were no longer subject to the terrible loneliness and isolation that an earlier generation of women had experienced. They knew that there were others with similar strivings in small communities and in large cities, who gathered at least annually in woman's rights conventions. This knowledge was of tremendous importance in producing the generation of female leaders who initiated the campaign for woman's rights and after decades of hard and bitter struggle carried it to fulfillment.

The Ideas Behind the Movement

A movement, in order to succeed, must have ideas which appeal to broad masses of people. The concepts of human equality and perfectability and of the right of the citizen to participate in government—ideas which powered the American and French Revolutions—inevitably influenced society's thinking in regard to women. The earliest and most comprehensive statement of feminism appeared in England in 1790 and reached America in 1792. Mary Wollstonecraft's *Vindication of the Rights of Women* had a decided influence on the popular American novelist Charles Brockden Brown, who felt inspired by it to write *Alcuin,* a tract setting forth ideas of female equality.

A generation of eighteenth-century revolutionaries from Voltaire to Thomas Paine, Benjamin Franklin, and Dr. Benjamin Rush, believing in the decisive influence of environment on the shaping of human destiny, had an equal faith in the potential intellectual equality of women, and spoke with conviction on their behalf. The contribution of Judith Sargent Murray, Mercy Warren, and Abigail Adams to this discussion have already been mentioned. Rationalist and egalitarian ideas were also brought to America by a number of visiting foreigners—Frances Wright, Harriet Martineau, and Frances Kemble.

Frances Wright's was the most important contribution. In her speeches, lectures, and articles, she developed between 1828 and 1834 a strong, logical, and coherent argument for woman's rights. As a rationalist, free-thinker, and confirmed revolutionary, she did not hesitate to develop her arguments to their ultimate extension: she advocated not only full equality for women, but also free love, birth control, and the right to divorce. She herself experienced a bitter divorce settlement: her husband, whom she had supported financially for over fifteen years, obtained every penny of her property and the custody of their child.

A similarly tragic divorce and public scandal involved Frances Kemble, a celebrated British actress who married Pierce Butler without realizing that he was a wealthy Georgian slave-holder. A brief stay on his plantation convinced her of the incompatibility of their views, and she asked for a divorce. Pierce Butler refused, and after a bitter and extended period of litigation Frances Kemble was deprived of her children and left without property, a living example of the humiliation the law could inflict on even the most educated and privileged woman.

Neither Frances Wright's nor Frances Kemble's advanced views drew much support from American women. On the contrary, Frances Wright's "bad reputation" and tragic personal fate were cited as a horrible example of feminine "notoriety" by a whole generation of American preachers and editorial writers.

While the influence of established religion generally tended to reinforce the ideas of woman's inferiority, contradictory trends appeared in the early nineteenth century. Revivalist ministers, preaching the need to translate religious conviction into practical reform activity, recommended the equal participation of women in revivalism and unleashed a tremendous source of female energy. The ideas that women were potentially the equal of men, and that they were morally obligated to strive for such equality, came out of this period of religious thought.

These ideas were most forcefully stated in what was the first fully developed feminist argument written by an American, Sarah Grimké's *Letters on the Equality of the Sexes,* which appeared in 1838. Sarah Grimké met the biblical arguments for the subordination of women head-on. She denied the Scriptures were divine in origin and pointed out that they were interpretations made by men of the word of God. She raised the moral argument for the equality of women and claimed: "God has made no distinction between men and women as moral beings. ... To me it is perfectly clear that *whatsoever it is morally right for a man to do, it is morally right for a woman to do.*" Sarah Grimké's largely theological discussion was followed in short order by a different type of argument from the pen of Margaret Fuller.

Margaret Fuller's *Woman in the Nineteenth Century* appeared in print in 1844. Her book was a much greater popular success than Sarah Grimké's, although its argument is less lucid. Margaret Fuller's claim for the equality of women was based on their intellect. Every woman had "the same divine energy as man" and must be free to develop as fully as man. "What Woman needs is ... as a nature to grow, as an intellect to discern, as a soul to live freely, and unimpeded to unfold such powers as were given her...." But Margaret Fuller agreed with Sarah Grimké and other feminist spokesmen that women were entitled to equal opportunities with men: "If you ask me what offices they may fill, I reply—any. I do not care what case you put; let them be sea captains if you will."

After Seneca Falls, the lone voices of individual rebels had become an organized chorus. Admittedly, the lofty Declaration of Principles drawn up at Seneca Falls had overstated the subjection of women considerably in order to arouse sympathy for the new cause. Perhaps not all of history was simply a history of "the subjection of woman by man," but to a growing number of women the issue presented itself rather simply. When Susan

B. Anthony was a self-supporting schoolteacher, her brother-in-law, in a typical expression of male prejudice, declared that he admired her for baking biscuits "rather than for solving Algebra problems." "There is no reason," Susan B. Anthony replied tartly, "why woman should not be able to do both." Many women saw the issue in these simple terms.

A Unique Team

It was the great good fortune of the American woman's rights movement to have produced two eminent leaders of very different talents whose fruitful collaboration extended over a period of almost fifty years. At the time Elizabeth Cady Stanton met young Susan B. Anthony in 1851, the Quaker schoolteacher was an abolitionist and active worker in temperance reform. It did not take Mrs. Stanton long to convert her to the cause of woman's rights, especially since Susan B. Anthony had already personally experienced discrimination as a schoolteacher.

Susan B. Anthony (1820–1906).   Susan B. Anthony was purposeful, straightlaced and lacking in humor. She was a poor writer, but had a marvelous ability to inspire others to work as unceasingly as she did. Her collaboration with Mrs. Stanton, to whom writing and felicity of expression came naturally, was of immense value to her, and gradually she became a most effective and accomplished speaker. Unmarried and free from domestic responsibility, Susan B. Anthony could provide the drive and energy both women needed if they were to accomplish their goal. Mrs. Stanton described their relationship in later years:

> We were at once fast friends, in thought and sympathy we were one, and in the division of labor we exactly complemented each other. In writing we did better work together than either could do alone. . . . I am the better writer, she the better critic. She supplied the facts and statistics, I the philosophy and rhetoric, and together we have made argu-

Elizabeth Cady Stanton (seated) and Susan B. Anthony

ments that have stood unshaken by the storms of thirty long years. . . . Our speeches may be considered the united product of our two brains.[18]

Throughout the years Susan B. Anthony provided a single-minded devotion and a practical politician's ability to keep her eye on essentials. Elizabeth Cady Stanton, more brilliant and creative, was also the more erratic of the two; she tended to embrace tangential issues and offend allies with her extreme views. Both women developed a stubborn disregard for the pressures of community and friends. Abuse, ridicule, slander, were an accepted part of their experience.

Mrs. Stanton built an elaborate argument for woman's rights; it was she who taught American women not only self-confidence, but a feeling of superiority. Woman, according to her, was in every potential equal to man, but in her moral sense she was his superior. Therefore she had a particular role to play in society, that of a regenerative force. However spurious this argument may sound to modern ears, it helped women overcome the sense of inferiority with which Victorian society had burdened them. Susan B. Anthony's main contribution was to build an organization which after seven decades of agitation, and despite factional splits and errors, achieved its major objective, the enfranchisement of women. "I have never lost my faith, not for a moment," she said at the age of eighty-five. "Failure is impossible."

Henry Stanton had his own ideas about this unusual teamwork. Once, handing his wife a sheaf of newspaper clippings he had collected concerning Susan B. Anthony's latest activities, he remarked: "Well, my dear, another notice of Susan. You stir up Susan and she stirs up the world."

Although both women failed to live to see the passage of the Nineteenth Amendment, which gave women the right to vote, their contribution to the development of American and world-wide feminism makes them major figures of our history.

PART THREE

From the Civil War to 1890

The Civil War, like all major wars, drew women in large numbers out of the home and into all aspects of economic life. In both the North and South, women organized and staffed the relief work for soldiers and prisoners of war, cared for the wounded, and helped to finance the commissioning of the troops. It was largely through female effort that supply, medical, and nursing services were established, which later became a permanent part of the armed forces. Thousands of women saw service as war nurses and helped to establish nursing as a profession.

The end of the war saw women firmly entrenched in several new fields of work, particularly office work, government service, and retail trade. Northern women in great numbers flocked to the South as teachers for the freedmen; later, southern women took their place in that region's newly-formed public schools. By the turn of the century, the majority of the nation's public school teachers were women. Associated with this development was the entry of women into higher education, the establishment of coeducational schools, women's colleges, and teacher training institutions, and the reluctant acceptance of some pioneering women in professional schools.

Urbanization, improved municipal services, and technological developments freed women from many of the tasks formerly performed in the home. Commercial production of food and clothing, the use of washing and sewing machines, and mechanization of home heating and lighting provided women with more leisure time. They used it to engage in cultural and civic activities outside of the home and thereby made important contributions to American life, including the establishment of playgrounds, parks, libraries, and settlement houses.

The period saw the spread of women's clubs, which provided the organizational base for the later growth of the woman's suffrage movement. Female reformers obtained leadership experience in broad-ranging efforts on behalf of the underprivileged, and began to make their political influence felt long before they obtained the ballot. Middle-class women organized by the millions and exerted pressure on all levels of government. Their concern was particularly pronounced in regard to temperance, the abolition of child labor, and the institutionalizing of welfare services for the poor, the handicapped, the orphaned, and the destitute.

At the other end of the social scale, tens of thousands of immigrant women and girls lived in poverty and misery in crowded tenements, and worked long hours for pitiful wages. Here family life was reduced to a desperate struggle for survival, as the home became a sweatshop in which children and their elders did piecework. Gradually, working girls organized in their own behalf, joined men in the embattled trade union movement, and participated in a number of strikes, in which they were supported by the more privileged feminist reformers.

For women of all classes, the home was no longer entirely the center of their lives. Families were now smaller and lived in smaller homes demanding less upkeep and care. With more than 20.6 percent of all women over 16 years of age gainfully employed in 1900, women no longer looked solely to their male relatives for support. The experience of working for wages gave them a new sense of independence and broadened their outlook. Lower-class women, in factory and trade union, developed a spirit of group solidarity and militancy and gave voice to new aspirations.

The social and economic developments of this period prepared the ground for the emergence of a strengthened woman's rights movement. They also decisively affected the life patterns and expectations of women. With a new century, a new woman was in the making.

CHAPTER EIGHT

Women in the Civil War

War, with its horrors, hardships, and abnormal conditions of life, is always a potent force for social change. Next to the slave, no group in society was more deeply affected by the Civil War than were American women.

From the beginning, women in both the North and South supported the war enthusiastically and expected it to end shortly in victory. They did a great deal to encourage recruitment, a significant action because at first both armies depended on volunteers.

Women helped to provision the soldiers and organized to collect, make, and distribute food and clothing. A few weeks after the outbreak of the war there were over 20,000 aid societies working for the soldiers on both sides. Enthusiasm and good will were great, and shirts, scarves, mittens, and socks flooded the volunteer soldiers. Ladies baked and cooked and hired teams of horses and wagons to carry home-made canned goods to the field. This unorganized enthusiasm naturally created chaos. Civilians and relief supplies often clogged the roads used by the military. Wagon-loads of food rotted by the wayside, while nearby soldiers went hungry. But the women soon learned from experience and saw the need for large-scale planning and organization.

Care of the Wounded

The Medical Department of the Union Army was totally unprepared for war. Its one military hospital had forty beds, no trained staff, and no means of transporting the wounded. Makeshift accommodations were improvised in hotels and boardinghouses near battlefields. There the wounded found little but crude shelter; no supplies, no trained nurses, and no proper food.

In April, 1861, some 3000 New York women, brought together through the efforts of Dr. Elizabeth Blackwell, organized the Woman's Central Association for Relief. It was the first organization of its kind in the United States and began immediately to train one hundred women as army nurses. It soon became evident that a national relief agency was necessary. In June, 1861, President Lincoln established the United States Sanitary Commission, headed by Henry Bellows. The Commission united the Woman's Central Association and other local aid societies, coordinated the care of Union soldiers, provided trained nurses, staffed and supplied hospitals, and organized transportation for the wounded. It spent in the course of the war the sum of $50,000,000, and most of this huge sum was raised through community Sanitary Fairs organized by women.

Dorothea Dix, the pioneer of medical reform, was appointed Superintendent of Nurses. Her strict regulations regarding nurses (only women over thirty and "plain in appearance" were accepted) and her arbitrary and inflexible manner created some resentment. But the difficulties she faced were enormous and were made even greater by the hostility of Army doctors, who feared the intrusion of women into their sphere and obstructed their work in every possible way. Still, order was created out of chaos and a modern medical service organized.

Work of the United States Sanitary Commission
during the Civil War

Much of the credit belongs to the remarkable women who, heroically and without acclaim, fought to make the situation of the wounded more tolerable. Society women like Georgeanna Woolsey, Louise Lee Schuyler, and Catherine Wormsley waded through blood and pus in filthy hospitals, scrubbed floors, foraged for food, and nursed the wounded. Mrs. Annie Wittenmyer pioneered in establishing army diet kitchens, which provided soft diets for the wounded who had previously been fed on salt pork and hardtack. Mrs. Mary Livermore worked as an organizer and fundraiser for the Sanitary Commission. Hundreds of lesser known women toiled endless hours in field stations and hospitals, braved infection and disease, and did a monumental job in support of their men.

The most legendary of these army nurses was a blunt, warmhearted widow, Mary Bickerdyke, known as "Mother" and beloved by thousands of soldiers. She served in General Sherman's army and became the terror of any inefficient, lazy, or drunken staff doctor or employee. She fought for "her boys" with the fierceness of a mother, met them with warm drinks and medical supplies as close as possible to the battle lines, and brought order into the inefficient administration of field hospi-

tals. She set up diet kitchens, laundries, bathtubs, and orderly nursing services. Once when she had secured the dismissal of a ward surgeon for his repeated drunkenness the man complained to General Sherman. When the General heard that the man had been accused by Mother Bickerdyke he said, "If it was she, I can't help you. . . . She ranks me."

Clara Barton, who nursed soldiers without an appointment by the Sanitary Commission, also saw the need for helping the wounded as soon as possible after injury. At Antietam, she arrived with an oxcart laden with medical supplies in the thick of the battle. She later made her greatest contribution by organizing the training of nurses and establishing the International and American Red Cross.

The Confederate Army was equally unprepared for wartime medical service. One of the first southern woman nurses was Sally Tompkins, who set up her own hospital in Richmond and was later commissioned a captain by the Confederacy. While resistance to women serving as nurses was even greater in the South than in the North, the need was also greater. In 1862 the Confederacy granted official status to women nurses. Mrs. Ella Newsom, a wealthy woman of social standing, became superintendent of an army hospital in Kentucky. Slaves and free Negro women also served in Confederate hospitals as nurses.

In all, at least 3200 women on both sides made a career of nursing in the Civil War. Hardships and male prejudice dogged their steps and pursued them even after the war. They had great difficulty in winning recognition for their services and many of them were left in want and ill health. It was only in 1892 that a bill was passed in Congress granting women Civil War nurses a pension of $12 a month. Yet the entry of women into nursing during the war was a turning point in making nursing a new profession for women.

Camp Followers and Spies

During the war many women became camp followers, respectably or otherwise. The wives of officers in both armies frequently visited their husbands and some even accompanied them. Many of the camp followers of the lower ranks did double duty as washerwomen, cooks and nurses. There was also a small, but adventuresome group who enlisted in male disguise. It is generally estimated that nearly four hundred women posed as soldiers and, for various lengths of time, served in the ranks. The most famous female Union soldier was Sarah Emma Edmonds, who served as a nurse, spy, courier, and soldier under the name of Franklin Thompson. She, like many of her kind, was discovered only when she became sick. She married after the war, but established her military rights satisfactorily and was given a veteran's pension in 1884.

The more romantic aspects of warfare were embodied in the female spies. These received much newspaper publicity, both during and after the war, and there is some doubt as to the authenticity of all of their exploits. Mrs. Rose O'Neal Greenhow, a Washington society hostess, was arrested and imprisoned for spying, but only after she had supplied the Confederate Army with important information contributing to their victory at the first battle of Bull Run. The Confederate spy Belle Boyd not only wormed military secrets out of her admirers, which she conveyed to the Confederate Army after daring midnight rides on horseback, but organized a spy ring in Virginia made up of teenage girls.

The Union, too, had its female spies. Pauline Cushman, a New Orleans actress who publicly toasted Jefferson Davis from the Louisville stage while active as a Union spy, was finally caught, sentenced to be executed, and then saved, in cliffhanger fashion, by the timely arrival of Union troops. Genteel Elizabeth Van Lew, playing the role of a harmless eccentric, rescued Union prisoners from Richmond prison right under the noses of the authorities, who made fun of "Crazy Bet" and her silly antics. Her pose was so successful that she was never molested, while she supplied General Grant steadily with military information. After the war she was rewarded by an appointment as postmistress of Richmond.

Union and Confederate women were also active as saboteurs, scouts, and couriers for both armies. They blew up bridges, cut

Harriet Tubman, Union scout and spy

telegraph wires, burned arsenals and warehouses, and helped prisoners to escape. Harriet Tubman, who was a nurse and cook in the Union Army throughout the war, is the only black woman known to have served also as a Union scout and spy.

A unique contribution was made by Anna Ella Carroll, the daughter of the former Governor of Maryland, a staunch Unionist trained in politics. Actively upholding the Union cause in the spring of secession, she performed valuable services as a political pamphleteer. Her other wartime services, as a military strategist, are somewhat controversial. She claimed, and several Senators supported the claim, that it was she who had suggested the plan followed in the Tennessee campaign by General Grant, which was one of the turning points of the war. She was known to have had free access to Lincoln's Cabinet, and it was claimed that she would have received her full due had Lincoln lived. However, since the idea of a woman suggesting military strategy would have been profoundly shocking to the nation and politically disastrous for the generals and the Republican party, recognition of her services was postponed, later disputed, and finally permanently deferred. In 1870 she filed a claim for compensation for her wartime services but never received recognition. She died poor and embittered.

Home Front Service

On the home fronts on both sides of the fighting line women stepped into the places left by men. They kept up farms and plantations, fed and clothed the civilians and helped to supply the soldiers. They worked in arsenals and munitions factories. More women than ever entered the mills of the North and, for the first time in history, women took their places in the offices of the Federal Government. The "government girls" were a controversial wartime innovation, but on both sides of the battle lines necessity triumphed over custom. Female government workers, like all female workers, had two things to recommend them: they were available in a period of severe manpower shortage, and they would work for less pay than the men.

For similar reasons women made great inroads during wartime in the fields of teaching, office work, and the retail trades, where they mostly worked as salesladies. In these trades, as well as in nursing, the gains made during the war were never quite lost in the postwar decades. Some women learned skilled trades such as printing, while others went into various businesses, and even banking. They also reestablished the preeminence of colonial women as keepers of boardinghouses and saloons. Moreover, a few women could be found in unusual occupations, working as steamboat captains, brokers, teamsters, or even morticians.

The South, cut off since the start of the war from most of the imports on which it had always depended, experienced serious shortages of all the necessities of life. Women therefore turned their homes and plantations into factories and workshops, reverting to the more primitive type of economy prevailing in colonial America.

Women of the South experienced the added horrors of a civil war fought on their own soil. Their towns and villages were battlegrounds; the wounded and dying collapsed on their doorsteps; occupying soldiers invaded their homes, seized their supplies and foodstuffs, and, not infrequently, set a torch to their houses. They saw their towns pillaged, their men carried off to northern prisons, their children grow thin for want of food. For them this was total war, their own war, a shattering, all-absorbing experience which destroyed all the mores and customs of generations. Under these circumstances southern women displayed heroic stamina and ingenuity in feeding themselves, their children, and their slaves.

"The woods, as well as being the great storehouse for all our dyestuffs, were also our drug stores," wrote Parthenia Hague, describing Civil War life in Alabama. "The berries of the dogwood tree were taken for quinine. . . . A soothing and efficacious cordial for dysentery and similar ailments was made from blackberry roots. . . ." The women substituted raspberry leaves for tea, toasted okra, yams, or bran for coffee, and discovered that ground corn cobs made an acceptable imitation baking soda. As one southern woman wrote:

All in our settlement learned to card, spin and weave. . . .

Our shoes, particularly those of women and children, were made of cloth . . . knit of homespun thread, either cotton or wool. . . . Sometimes we put on the soles ourselves by taking worn out shoes . . . ripping the soles off, placing them in warm water to make them more pliable and to make it easier to pick out all the old stitches, and then in the same perforations stitching our knit slippers or cloth-made shoes. . . .

Sewing societies were formed in every hamlet, as well as in our cities to keep the soldiers of the Confederacy clothed as best we could. . . . To such societies all the cloth that could be spared from each household was given and made into soldiers' garments. . . .

In many settlements there were spinning "bees." Wheels, cards and cotton were all hauled in a wagon to the place appointed. . . . Sometimes as many as six or eight wheels would be whirring at the same time in one house. . . . We were drawn together in a closer union, a tenderer feeling of humanity linking us all together, both rich and poor.[19]

Inflation, ruthless war profiteering, irregular pay to soldiers, and the total absence of family allotments in both the North and South made the life of the poorer civilians a daily struggle for survival. Many soldiers' wives, in desperation, appealed to their husbands for help. One poor woman from Virginia, mother of four small children, wrote this pathetic letter to her husband:

Dec. 17, 1864

. . . Christmus is most hear again, and things is worse and worse. . . . Everything me and children's got is patched. . . . We haven't got nothing in the house to eat but a little bit o' meal. I don't want you to stop fighten them yankees till you kill the last one of them, but try and get off and come home and fix us all up some and then you can go back and fight them a heep harder. . . . We can't

103

none of us hold out much longer down here . . . my dear
if you put off a-comin' 'twon't be no use to come, for we'll
all hands of us be out there in the garden in the old grave-
yard with your ma and mine.[20]

The husband responded by going home without leave. On
his return he was arrested, tried as a deserter, and sentenced to
be executed. Luckily for him, there were so many similar cases
in the Confederate Army that a general amnesty for deserters
was declared.

Protest and Violence.   Poor women in both the North and
South protested, petitioned, and, when all else failed, rioted.
Bread riots, usually made up of the half-starved, ragged mothers and wives of volunteers, swept the cities as the war deep-
ened. The most spectacular and violent of these took place in
New York City, New Orleans and Atlanta. The terrible New
York draft riots of 1863, which started as a protest against the
hiring of substitutes for conscripted soldiers and turned into a
race riot, saw women behaving as violently as men. Irish laborers, too poor to pay for substitutes and fearful they would be
replaced by black workers if drafted, formed a mob that hunted
down and killed blacks, pillaged and burned homes, and for
three days terrorized the city. Women took part in the looting
and even in the killing and some of them were killed. Several
hundred women were arrested and many found guilty. The fact
that women participated in such violence was deeply shocking
to contemporaries, but war conditions served to remove normal
restraints of custom and propriety and to bring out the worst
as well as the best in men and women.

The women who had been in the woman's rights movement
before the war temporarily suspended their agitation for their
special interests in order to support the "slave's cause." Shortly
after Lincoln issued his Emancipation Proclamation, the feminists formed the National Woman's Loyal League, an organization with a single goal—the circulation of a petition to Congress
asking for a constitutional amendment ending slavery in the
United States. During the campaign, seasoned speakers like
Elizabeth Cady Stanton and the spectacularly successful new-

104

comer, Anna Dickinson, rallied public support in hundreds of meetings for the future Thirteenth Amendment. The women finally obtained 400,000 signatures on their petition.

In all areas touching the lives of women—family, home, work, politics—the war disrupted life, shattered tradition, and created change. Southern women, especially, were forced out of their sheltered homes and into new roles as breadwinners, educators, and reformers. While many women gladly returned to the tranquility of their prewar lives as soon as they could, society as a whole had seen women in new and unaccustomed roles. In this, as in so many other ways, the Civil War marked a watershed in American history. Women would never be quite the same again.

CHAPTER NINE

The Educated Woman in a Period of Transition

Even while the battles of the Civil War were still raging, the plight of the freed slaves who were flocking as "contraband" to the Union armies and as refugees into the cities became a matter of serious concern. Voluntary aid societies were unable to provide for the millions of refugees. Early in 1865, in response to abolitionist pressure, Congress created the Freedmen's Bureau to provide relief and employment for the former slaves.

Freedmen's Relief and Schooling

The Freedmen's Bureau undertook the complex job of coordinating the work of voluntary aid societies, feeding and housing refugees, schooling them, finding them jobs, and protecting them from ex-Confederate terrorists. The Bureau was highly controversial, constantly embattled, and short-lived. Yet in the five years of its existence it aided millions of black and white

Southerners, saved thousands from starvation, and, as its most lasting contribution, laid the foundation of Negro education in the South. The Freedmen's Bureau constructed hundreds of schoolhouses, provided salaries for teachers, and created a public school system that benefited both black and white children. By 1869 over 9000 teachers were at work in the black schools of the South. Most of these were women; a third of them southern white women forced into this employment by economic need. Others were idealistic northern women who came to the South to teach the freedmen and persisted for many years in the face of great difficulties and much hostility from the white community. Laura Towne, a white teacher from Massachusetts, and Charlotte Forten, a Philadelphia Negro woman, were among those who have left moving accounts of their experiences during this period.

Josephine Griffing (1814–1872).   The most dynamic advocate of relief work among the freedmen was Josephine Griffing. Born in Connecticut, she moved with her husband to the Western Reserve of Ohio, where both were active in abolition, temperance, and feminist societies. Josephine Griffing joined a small group of women who pioneered as public lecturers, and during the war was an organizer for the petition campaign of the National Woman's Loyal League. In 1864 she became the general agent of the National Freedmen's Relief Association of the District of Columbia, a post she occupied until her death. She raised a great deal of money for the destitute refugees flocking into Washington, lobbied on their behalf, and helped to set up a number of benevolent institutions. She operated two industrial schools for women and children which established the educational patterns followed later at Hampton and Tuskegee Institutes. She also organized workshops in which poor women could learn the needle trades. Her Washington headquarters became a sort of early settlement house in which the freedmen could find temporary shelter, relief, counseling, workshops, and training.

Josephine Griffing was especially interested in helping the resettlement of freedmen in the western and northern states. She personally helped to settle between three and five thousand of them. She was among the few people foresighted enough to understand that the only permanent solution to the problem of the freed slaves would be to grant them land. She lobbied for this idea extensively, but did not prevail. In the later years of her life Mrs. Griffing was disheartened by the growing indifference toward the destitute, aged, and often helpless freedmen in northern cities, but she continued to work actively for them until her death.

The Negro's, Not the Woman's Hour

During the war the feminists had subordinated their own interests to an all-out effort on behalf of emancipation. Afterwards they expected the full support of abolitionists for the inclusion of woman's rights in civil rights legislation. In this they were bitterly disappointed. Reconstruction legislation was controversial, and its supporters did not wish to endanger its passage by attaching to it an unpopular cause such as female suffrage. Even such a staunch supporter of woman's rights as Frederick Douglass proclaimed loudly that this was "the Negro's hour." The Fourteenth and Fifteenth Amendments did not outlaw sex discrimination. Many feminists, indeed, thought that the Fourteenth Amendment actually worsened the legal status of American women. The Constitution had never contained any specific restriction against female suffrage, and the matter had been left to the states. The Fourteenth Amendment, however, guaranteed "male inhabitants" the vote and specifically mentioned "male citizens," thus enshrining sex discrimination in federal law.

The issue caused a serious split in the feminist movement. In 1869 Susan B. Anthony and Elizabeth Cady Stanton set up the National Woman Suffrage Association, which excluded men from membership and pushed for a single goal of a constitutional amendment granting suffrage to women. The American Woman Suffrage Association, led by Henry Blackwell, Lucy

Lucy Stone

Stone, Julia Ward Howe, and Mary Livermore, was established to work for the same goal through state organization.

Lucy Stone (1818–1893).   The American Woman Suffrage Association brought the third of the great leaders of the early feminist movement into a position of national leadership. Unlike Elizabeth Cady Stanton and Susan B. Anthony, Lucy Stone had been a feminist before becoming an abolitionist. After teaching school and graduating from Oberlin, she spent many years as a lecturer on woman's rights and abolition. After the war, she set out to build a feminist organization of both men and women. To counteract the Stanton-Anthony journal, *The Revolution,* Lucy Stone founded *The Woman's Journal,* which she, her husband, and later her daughter edited.

Leaders of both wings of the suffrage movement participated in the ill-fated Kansas suffrage referendum of 1867, in which both Negro and female suffrage were decisively defeated. But the leaders of the "American" were undaunted in their determination to secure the franchise by winning it state by state.

The split in the woman's rights movement continued for over twenty years and greatly weakened it. But even a unified feminist movement would probably not have gained the suffrage during this period, because other issues were taking priority in the public mind. Women, as well as men, were more absorbed with the great changes wrought in their society by industrialization, and with taking advantage of technological innovations and educational opportunities. These proved to be of more lasting significance in changing the status of women than the organized movement for suffrage.

Advances in the Professions and the Arts

The female teacher had become accepted, both in the North and South, during and shortly after the Civil War. In 1860 about twenty-five percent of the nation's elementary and secondary teachers were women. By 1880, the figure was sixty percent, by

Women students in chemistry laboratory of
Massachusetts Institute of Technology

1910, eighty percent. The necessity of training this vast army of female teachers led to the spread of normal schools and teacher training institutions and to the continued pressure on schools of higher education to admit women.

Between 1865 and 1890 a number of women's colleges were founded, among them Vassar, Smith, Wellesley, Bryn Mawr, Barnard, and Radcliffe. Land grant colleges had been coeducational ever since 1862. As universities increasingly began to accept women, the pressure for graduate training grew. This in turn created new administrative and executive jobs for women in female colleges. The appointment and advancement of women to administrative jobs in coeducational colleges had to wait for a later day.

The Medical Field.   The disheartening struggle of a few pioneering women who were admitted to medical training before the Civil War had opened the doors to the new generation. New York Medical College, established by Dr. Elizabeth Blackwell, and the Woman's Medical College of Chicago provided training opportunities for female physicians. In 1871 the University of Michigan Medical School admitted female students, although they were put in segregated classes. By the 1890's more than a

dozen medical schools were coeducational, and professional societies admitted women doctors to membership.

A number of Civil War nurses went on to become physicians, while others struggled to stay in nursing in civilian life. Gradually, nursing schools patterned after the London Nightingale School began to elevate the age-old occupation of women, which had been regarded as little more than an extension of domestic service, into a profession. Academic standards were raised and the training period lengthened to three years. Clara Barton's immense contribution in organizing the American Red Cross further elevated the status of the nursing profession. There were 1100 "trained nurses" listed in the 1900 census, most of them working on private cases.

Science. In 1850, when the American Academy of Arts and Sciences (AAAS) elected astronomer Maria Mitchell to membership, her achievement was considered remarkable not only because she was an accomplished scientist, who had discovered a comet which bears her name, but because she was the first woman elected to this distinguished scientific society.

It took thirty-five years before another woman was found worthy of such an honor. Erminnie A. Smith, a former pupil of Emma Willard, was a geologist and ethnologist notable for her studies of Iroquois Indian culture and for her work in compiling an Iroquois-English dictionary. Her graduate training in Germany had also made her a distinguished geologist and botanist. A mother of four children, she became a Fellow of the AAAS in 1885 and the organization's first female officer, secretary of the anthropology section. But a full breakthrough of women in the scientific professions only came when the next generation of college-trained women beat down the prejudices against admission into graduate schools.

Ministry and the Law. In other professions, the struggle was yet to be won. Antoinette Brown was the first woman minister to preach, though briefly, before the Civil War. After the war, Dr. Anna Howard Shaw, already a licensed preacher and college graduate, entered Boston University to study for a theological degree. She was the only woman among forty-two young men studying for the ministry, and found not only social

Maria Mitchell (seated)

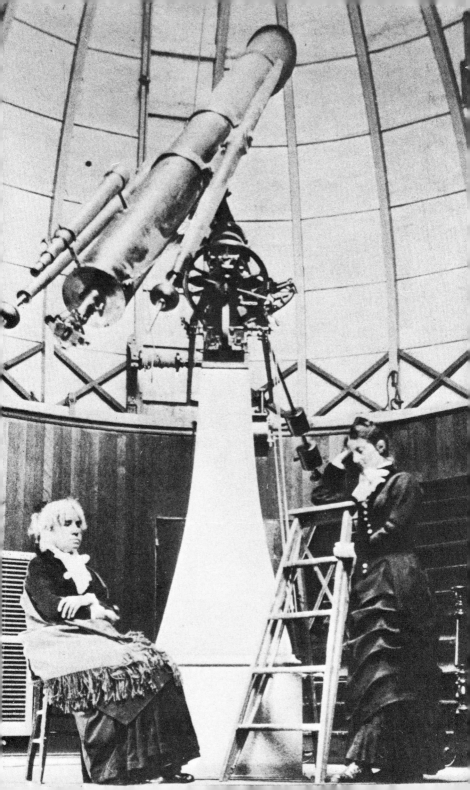

discrimination but great economic hardship. Although by the end of the century some of the Protestant denominations admitted women to the ministry, most churches excluded them from the ministerial profession and many do so to this day.

State courts controlled the licensing of lawyers and, by precedent and common practice, excluded women. One of the first to attempt a legal career was Mrs. Myra Bradwell. In 1870 her application to practice law was denied by the Illinois Supreme Court on the ground that "this step . . . would mean . . . that it is in harmony with the Constitution and laws that women should be made governors, judges, and sheriffs," an assumption the court was not as yet prepared to endorse. Mrs. Bradwell carried her appeal to the Supreme Court where she also lost, but the agitation connected with her case led the Illinois legislature to pass a law in 1872 abolishing sex discrimination in employment.

Meanwhile other states had permitted women to practice law. Phebe W. Couzins, the first female graduate of Washington University in St. Louis, was licensed to practice in Missouri. Charlotte Ray, graduate of Howard University, was the first black woman lawyer. The Supreme Court of the United States refused Belva Lockwood, a practicing lawyer in Washington, D.C., permission to practice before it unless and until "such a change is required by statute." Mrs. Lockwood, in five years of lobbying, succeeded in winning enough Senate support for passage of just such a bill, and in 1879 she was admitted to practice before the Supreme Court.

Although discrimination against women was weakening in most of the professions by the turn of the century, only a few women gained professional status. The difficulties and social disapproval facing them were sufficient to keep most women from such careers. One of the by-products of this struggle was the formation of sex-segregated professional training schools and societies.

Literature.   Writing had been one of the earliest fields open to women and, because of its private and secluded nature, had long offered an outlet for female talent. The tradition of female authorship of best-selling fiction, which started at the time of the founding of the republic, continued unabated after the Civil War. Sentimental poets of doubtful talent filled the pages of the mass circulation magazines and lady journalists proliferated. They were avidly read by contemporaries; their earnings were often sizeable, and their outpourings have been mercifully forgotten.

Yet the great poet of her age and possibly the greatest American poet of all time was unknown, unread, and unrewarded during her lifetime. Her lonely and eccentric figure is unique among women in American history, both for the quality of her life and for her genius.

Emily Dickinson (1830–1886).   Outwardly Emily Dickinson lived the circumscribed life of a typical nineteenth-century spinster. With the exception of a few brief trips and one year in boarding school, she never left her native village of Amherst, Massachusetts. Most of her youth was spent in the dutiful pursuit of domesticity—baking bread and making puddings, attending her demanding father, and caring for her invalid mother. After her parents' death, she lived in quiet and genteel retirement with her sister, Lavinia. In childhood she was a charming and outgoing girl, intelligent, fun-loving and fond of the outdoors, but with a tendency to sudden fits of depression. A year at Mount Holyoke Female Seminary left her unhappy because she did not share in the religious enthusiasm so strongly inculcated in the students by the dynamic Mary Lyon.

There is little known about the events that transformed her from the normal and outgoing young woman with many girl friends and "gentlemen callers" to the recluse of later years. There are suggestions that she was disappointed in love, that she was rejected by an older married man with whom she fe'l in love, that her father's demanding behavior frightened off potential suitors, or that she was struggling with severe depressions. In any case something, perhaps a combination of several of these conjectured events, led finally to her retiring from society. Neither she nor her sister Lavinia married, and the choices open to unmarried small-town girls such as they were in fact very restricted. But Emily Dickinson turned inward and made of her enforced "imprisonment" a rare and challenging adventure. At the age of thirty-one she began to write poetry and for the rest of her life poured all her intensity of feeling and sensibility into her work.

That her poetry was almost lost to posterity and went totally unrecognized during her lifetime was perhaps in large measure due to the position of women in her time as much as to her own reticence. While inferior talents were readily published in the pages of the magazines and journals, there was little precedent for the serious woman poet to find recognition, except among her own kind. It is perhaps no accident that the two people to whom she confided her artistic work were both connected with reform. Her friend Helen Hunt Jackson made an impassioned plea for justice for the Indian in her novel *Ramona.* And the man whom Emily Dickinson called "my dear preceptor" and to whom she sent most of her work, not so much for criticism as for an audience reaction, was Thomas Wentworth Higginson, an abolitionist reformer and staunch pioneer for women's rights. Higginson has been blamed by many literary critics for not encouraging Dickinson to publish during her lifetime, but there is good evidence that it was she who refused to be published. At all events Higginson, in their many years of correspondence, provided sufficient echo and encouragement to sustain Emily Dickinson in her work, and he had the perception to respect her unusual talent and to preserve everything she sent to him. After her death it was he who, together with Mabel Loomis Todd, edited and published her poems, which led to almost instant acclaim of her genius.

Emily Dickinson's shadowy form, clad always in white, usually carrying a flower, moving noiselessly from room to room, has intrigued biographers and historians. She herself remains impenetrably mysterious, but her work speaks clearly. Her acute sense of observation was, like Thoreau's, trained to the perception in depth of the world of nature—flowers, birds, children, and the inner self. As Van Wyck Brooks said in his *New England: Indian Summer; 1865–1915,* she lived in "a world of paradox . . . her eye was microscopic, her imagination dwelled with mysteries and grandeurs . . . her poems . . . packed with meaning were fairylike in their shimmering lightness . . .

and yet one felt behind them an imagery of mind and spirit that only the rarest poets possess."

The tightness of her language, the brilliance of her imagery, the intensity of her feeling, and the originality of her concepts make her unique among American literary figures, and can find their likeness only in the work of such poets as William Blake.

Women novelists at the turn of the century were preoccupied with finely wrought, sensitively observed regional fiction. Sarah Orne Jewett (1849–1909) detailed the life and the people of rural Maine in several of her books and sketches, the best known of which is *Country of the Pointed Firs.* Ellen Glasgow, a southern writer, and Willa Cather, who depicted the harsh life on the midwestern prairie, were typical of the best of this regional fiction writing. Edith Wharton described the dying aristocracy of New York society. All four of these writers were characterized by superb craftsmanship, acute observation, and nostalgia for a time and society passing out of existence. The rough and tumble of social criticism in an age of change was best represented by the journalist, Ida M. Tarbell, whose exposé of the Standard Oil Company is one of the classics of "muck-raking literature." Emma Lazarus, mostly remembered for her poem inscribed on the Statue of Liberty, wrote of Jewish themes.

The period of the Gilded Age saw the emergence of women intellectuals in various fields. They were still rare enough to be considered pioneers, but it was obvious that times were changing and that the ideas of the early nineteenth century were no longer relevant to women in the age of industrialization and mass education. The "new woman" was about to be born.

CHAPTER TEN

Women Organize for Community Betterment

Technological developments of the post-Civil War years freed women from much of the drudgery of housework. Improvements in gas lighting, municipal water supplies, and plumbing made housekeeping easier and more efficient. The development of canning and of packaged foods and the commercial production of bread and cereals shortened the time the housewife had to spend in cooking. Improved laundry and cooking facilities and the popularization of the sewing machine further lightened domestic chores, while more and more of the tasks formerly performed in the home were now performed in factories. The result was that increasing numbers of women had leisure time to spend in other pursuits and to develop their talents in new ways.

Club Women

Julia Ward Howe, wife of a physician and outstanding medical reformer, an educated woman who read Greek, Latin, and German philosophy, was the prototype of the new lady of leisure.

She is remembered mainly as the author of "The Battle Hymn of the Republic," but her major contribution was as a club woman. In 1868, together with other Boston women, she founded the New England Women's Club, whose president she was for many years. During the same year, the Sorosis Club was founded in New York. Very soon, similar organizations sprang up in Chicago, San Francisco, and other cities, combining in 1890 to form the General Federation of Women's Clubs. These early women's clubs ranged far and wide in their interests. Always centers of cultural and literary activity, they were also much concerned with improving social conditions in their own communities.

For many, of course, club life performed merely a social function. Others looked to it for self-improvement or saw it as a field in which they could make themselves useful and gain some importance and renown. To the many farm women who organized through the Grange, their clubs were a means of keeping in touch with the women of other regions and of combatting their often painfully felt isolation.

No group had more reason to organize than did black women who, by painstaking effort and hard work, struggled to elevate not only themselves and their families, but their communities. Ever since the Civil War they had staffed the segregated schools of the South, where the threat of violence and lynching was an ever-present reality. Ida Wells Barnett, born in Mississippi during the Civil War, conducted a one-woman crusade against lynching. Orphaned, she supported her four brothers and sisters by teaching school from the time she was fourteen years old. Later she became part-owner and editor of the *Memphis Free Speech,* a Negro newspaper. Her attacks on the inferior, segregated schools for black children led to her dismissal from the Memphis school system. In 1892, she exposed the economic motive behind the lynching of three black storekeepers in Memphis. For this bold attack her newspaper office was mobbed, her life was threatened, and she was warned not to return to town. She responded by publishing a detailed record and exposé of the lynchings of the period 1892–1894, and became a lecturer on this subject, both in the United States and abroad. She also helped to organize black women's clubs in various cities and anti-lynching societies in England.

The organization of clubs, which for white women was a matter of choice and, at times, diversion, was a matter of necessity for black women. They recognized that the enormous difficulties they had to surmount required organized strength. Mrs. Josephine St. Pierre Ruffin and Mrs. Booker T. Washington were leading forces in these early organizing efforts. Under their leadership the women's clubs of various cities were merged, in 1896, into the National Association of Colored Women, headed by Mrs. Mary Church Terrell. Concerned with moral uplift, education, and social services as much as their white counterparts, the women in the black clubs has to suffer the indignity of being admitted to the General Federation of Women's Clubs only in segregated locals. The colored women's clubs became a training ground for leadership, a link between the educated elite and the general mass, and an important force in community betterment.

For the black woman the struggle against race prejudice was a constant, overwhelming necessity. Conversely, each gain, each new step toward dignity and achievement became a matter of pride for the whole race. The two outstanding black women leaders of this period personified the preoccupation with personal achievement and betterment of the race. Both were dynamic, forceful personalities, gifted, dedicated, and able to bridge the gap between the black and white worlds.

Mary McLeod Bethune (1875–1955). Raised in great poverty on a cotton farm in South Carolina, Mary McLeod Bethune always remained close to her southern country roots, even when she became the first member of her race to head a federal agency. A scholarship student at Scotia Seminary and graduate of Moody Bible Institute in Chicago, she taught school in several southern states after her graduation in 1895. She married Albertus Bethune, a schoolteacher, in 1898, and had one son, but later separated from her husband.

In 1904 she started a school with five girls, building a rough shed on an abandoned town dump and raising money for materials and books by selling sweet potato pies she and her

Maria McLeod Bethune and children

students baked each night. Through the unceasing efforts and perseverance of its founder, Daytona Normal and Industrial Institute for Girls grew from these humble beginnings into Bethune Cookman College, a well-endowed coeducational institution, annually graduating nearly one thousand students. Mrs. Bethune served as its president until 1942.

As president of the National Association of Colored Women's Clubs and of its Florida state affiliate, her leadership embraced ever widening circles. She became active on the national scene in the 1920's and 1930's as vice-president of the NAACP and was a leading spirit in the movement toward interracial cooperation of southern women. She was appointed director of the Division of Negro Affairs of the National Youth Administration, a position she held from 1936 to 1944, and served as special consultant on Negro affairs to President Franklin D. Roosevelt. She was special assistant to the Secretary of War in 1942 and a member of the twelve-man Commission for National Defense appointed by President Harry S. Truman in 1951.

At national and international conferences and conventions, she became a symbol of race achievement. Standing up quietly for her rights, she shamed bigots and weathered innumerable affronts by her personal dignity. Her high office and wide influence never lessened her deep commitment to the poor people from whom she came and to the militant pursuit of full citizenship rights for all black Americans.

Mary Church Terrell (1863–1954). One of the earliest black graduates from Oberlin College was Mary Church Terrell, who graduated in 1884 and, like so many other college-trained women, went on to teaching. In 1895 she became the first black woman member of the Washington, D.C., Board of Education, a position she held for sixteen years. A convinced suffragist, she attended and spoke at a number of suffrage conventions. From 1895 on, as president of the National Association of Colored Women, she was the outstanding spokesman for black women. A militant civil rights advocate, she organized picket lines and sit-ins in the 1930's and 1940's and won a major victory in her campaign to desegregate the restaurants in the nation's capital. The refusal of the American Association of University Women to accept her membership in 1949 caused nationwide protest, and led to a change in that organization's by-laws and practices.

In working for any local reform, club women, black and white, came up against the power structure of their communities. They learned that it took more than a convincing argument to influence the business leaders and politicians to make necessary reforms. More and more women became convinced of the necessity of participating in politics and of the need for suffrage. In no field of reform was this more spectacularly demonstrated than in the temperance movement.

The Temperance Movement

The temperance movement had been church-connected all through the early nineteenth century. Women were interested in this cause for very practical reasons. It was tragic to have an alcoholic in the family, in view of the total legal and economic dependency of wives on their husbands. The fear of drunkenness was thus very real to many women.

The Woman's Christian Temperance Union (WCTU), formed in 1874, grew out of a movement of local "praying bands" of women who temporarily succeeded in closing thousands of saloons in the Middle West by holding prayer meetings on the premises. The exploits of Carrie Nation, who invaded saloons with an axe to smash the bottles and glasses, have made this cause appear ridiculous and fanatic. It was that, but it was more. At a time when the woman's suffrage movement was split and weakened, the temperance movement became an organizational school for hundreds of thousands of women. Frances Willard, who shortly after the founding of the WCTU became its moving spirit, must be credited with turning the pet cause of a small group of zealots into the most dynamic women's organization the country had ever seen.

Frances Willard (1839–1898).   Born in New York and raised in the West, Frances Willard enjoyed an excellent education. After a decade of teaching, she became president of Evan-

123

ston Female College in Illinois. She resigned from the job because of administrative disagreements and shortly afterwards began her work with the WCTU, which she served as national secretary until her death.

She proposed that woman's suffrage be added to the WCTU's program and won out over the opposition of more conservative leadership, convincing women that they could not protect their homes from liquor without having a voice in public affairs. She saw the organization as a means for uniting women across the country, and took pride in seeing black and white southern women taking their first steps toward cooperation in WCTU meetings.

Her slogan was "Do everything," and she applied it literally. The WCTU provided for paid organizers at the national, state, and local level, and set an example of businesslike organization. The work itself touched upon every aspect of community life. Textbooks and educational materials were provided for public schools and churches. Each city was urged to purchase and run its own temperance tabernacle and alcohol-free restaurant. Parlor meetings were arranged for influential citizens, tea parties for mothers, boys' clubs for orphans; no detail was overlooked. Women provided free lunches at the polls on election day, complete with temperance literature and pledges. Girls were taught hygiene, diet, dress reform, and the arts of homemaking. The WCTU initiated industrial and reform schools for girls, homes for alcoholic women, and evening schools for working girls. It concerned itself with such minor improvements as the installation of public drinking fountains. It campaigned for the introduction of hygiene instruction in the public schools, and for the employment of policewomen. Suffrage and legislative work were stressed on a year-round basis.

The mass appeal of Frances Willard's approach is shown by the spectacular growth of the organization. Starting with a few hundred in 1874, the WCTU in 1892 had 10,000 local groups organized in every state and county. They issued newspapers, owned buildings and businesses, and had an active membership of 200,000, with almost as many youths organized in separate juvenile groups.

Small wonder that the liquor interests became more emphatic in their opposition to woman suffrage. This later led to heated debates between temperance and suffrage leaders who thought that the WCTU did more harm than good to their cause. After the death of Frances Willard in 1898, the WCTU gradually reduced its aims to the original one of temperance, but it is certain that no other organization reached and influenced so many women in the nineteenth century.

The Settlement Houses

By 1900 there were six cities of more than a half million population in the United States, and three of them had a population of over a million. While during most of the century most Americans had lived in rural areas, the last two decades of the nineteenth century saw more and more people moving to the city and engaging in industrial pursuits. By 1890 the number of industrial wage earners in the country was almost as large as that of farm owners, tenants, and farm laborers combined. In these same decades, unprecedented numbers of immigrants from Europe poured into the eastern seaboard cities. In the 1880's five and a quarter million entered the country each year; in the next decade the figure was three and three-quarter million.

This influx of mainly poor people into the city, from rural America and from abroad, led to the crowding of people into the poorer parts of cities and the creation of large slum areas. Inevitably, in the overcrowded slums and tenements, crime, corruption, and vice flourished. Charity workers of the old kind were helpless to discover who among the "depraved classes" was worthy of their charitable support. Wretchedness, degradation, exploitation, and misery were everywhere, and for the first time middle-class reformers began to see the need for understanding the causes of such conditions, rather than simply trying to alleviate them. Out of this need arose the settlement house movement, which became a great force for reform and social improvement.

Jane Addams (1860–1935).   Like many another reformer, Jane Addams grew up in a cultured and sheltered environment, in which she gradually came to feel dissatisfied and useless. Deeply touched by the wretchedness she saw among the poor of London on a European trip, she studied British settlement houses and became determined to carry out a similar experiment in America. In 1889 she moved with her furnishings, pictures, and books into Hull-House on Halstead Street in Chicago to "share the lives of the poor." Jane Addams believed that charity should work by example, not by condescension, and persuaded other young women of middle-class backgrounds to join her at Hull-House to give what service they could to people of the neighborhood. Armed only with unbounded idealism, faith in the goodness of all human beings, and a practical and pragmatic approach toward self-help, the settlement house workers braved the challenge of the slums. Their greatest asset was genuine sympathy for the people they worked with and a sense of long-term commitment. They believed that only through a shared life could they gain the confidence of their neighbors and in time "help them to express themselves and make articulate their desires."

The settlement workers' approach to community work was to measure their success by the degree to which they were able to put themselves out of business. Inevitably their reforming efforts brought them face to face with the established powers in the city and with the politicians. As Jane Addams wrote:

> Unsanitary housing, poisonous sewage, contaminated water, infant mortality, the spread of contagion, adulterated food, impure milk, smoke-laden air, ill-ventilated factories, dangerous occupations, juvenile crime, unwholesome crowding, prostitution and drunkenness are the enemies which the modern city must face and overcome would it survive.[21]

Settlement workers pressured city administrators for a variety of reforms, from improved garbage collection to public programs for health and sanitation. They prodded private charities

126

Jane Addams and children

into making needed contributions. They persuaded libraries to open branches in the slums, and art museums to remain open longer hours and provide exhibits in poor neighborhoods. They badgered and labored until slum children could be sent on summer vacations to camps in the country. They also became concerned with the more deep-seated causes of poverty and attacked the sweatshop system, the exploitation of women, child labor, the miserable wages paid to unorganized workers, and other such evils. Before long they were to be found among the staunchest advocates of labor reforms such as the eight-hour day, unionization, and minimum wage legislation.

Settlement workers demanded municipal regulation of housing and sanitation; they endorsed woman suffrage as a means of making women more effective "in the housekeeping of public life." They advocated welfare payments for the needy, unemployment compensation, and social insurance. Fanning out into every area that touched the lives of the poor, settlement house workers became a potent force for social change.

The interests of Jane Addams and her associates and followers ranged far and wide, embracing all social problems from the proper nutrition of immigrant children to the issue of world peace, which became one of Jane Addams' absorbing interests in the later years of her life. But perhaps the most significant function of the settlement house movement was that of a training ground for future leaders of various reforms. Out of Hull-House came such reform leaders as Florence Kelley, Mary Simkovitch, Lillian Wald, and Grace Abbott. Mary Anderson, a shoe worker and leader of her union, long remembered the meetings held at Hull-House. "For me," she said, "and for many others, Hull-House and Jane Addams opened the door to a larger life." Based on the Hull-House model, over fifty settlement houses were founded in the northern and eastern cities.

Reformers became specialists in their attack upon the evils of the city. Many women were particularly interested in the protection of consumers. The pioneer and outstanding leader in this field was Florence Kelley, for thirty-two years the secretary and moving spirit of the National Consumers League. She was one of the women who effected basic changes in American life by combining a passionate sympathy for the downtrodden with a cool and practical realism in using organization and political pressure to achieve her objectives.

The Consumers League not only demanded consumer protection but enlisted the support of shoppers in helping to improve the conditions of workers. Educational campaigns and selective boycotts were used to pressure businesses to abolish child labor and alleviate the exploitation of women workers. Florence Kelley had the ability to attract outstanding reformers from various fields to these causes—settlement workers like Grace and Edith Abbott, Jane Addams, Josephine and Pauline Goldmark, Lillian Wald, Alice Hamilton; wealthy society women who became interested in the welfare of the poor, such as Emily Balch, Maud Nathan, Eleanor Roosevelt; and a remarkable group of male reformers, Louis Brandeis, John R. Commons, Paul Kellogg, John H. Lathrop.

The Protection of Children

The long struggle for the abolition of child labor, in which the National Consumer League had pioneered, led to the establishment of the National Child Labor Committee in 1904. For over thirty years the Committee battled on the educational, legal, and legislative fronts to end the exploitation of children. The chief objective of the reformers, the outlawing of child labor, was only accomplished with the passage of the Fair Labor Standards Act in 1938. In the course of this long and difficult struggle, many peripheral goals were achieved: the establishment of the United States Children's Bureau in 1912; the convening of White House conferences on children every decade; the setting of minimum standards for health and safety of employed youths; free medical and dental care in school; school lunches; reductions in infant mortality and maternal death rates; local and state recreation programs; and aid to "special" children, the crippled, handicapped, mentally retarded, and emotionally disturbed.

One aspect of this reform activity was the concept of aid to orphaned and dependent children through widow's pensions and, later, through federal grants. Sophie Loeb, a Jewish immigrant from Russia who herself had experienced the devastating effects of the death of a father on the destitute widow and young orphans, became the inspired leader of this cause. A professional reporter, Sophie Loeb campaigned for years for widows' pensions, so that mothers might stay home to care for their children instead of sending them to orphanages. In her decades of campaigning she became a recognized expert on international law and welfare measures pertaining to children. She finally saw victory in the enactment of the first Mother's Pension Bill in New York State in 1915. Appointed president of the Board of Child Welfare, she demonstrated that home care for dependent children was more humane, more effective, and no more costly than institutional care. Her concern embraced every aspect of child welfare, and she succeeded in promoting playgrounds, child lunch programs, and various reforms designed to improve the lot of illegitimate children. "Not charity but a chance for every child" was the slogan that inspired her to action on behalf of American children.

The leadership and organized efforts of women in voluntary reform organizations were an immense contribution to the building of a society dedicated to the ideal of individual freedom, economic security, and equal opportunity. The reformers were quite aware of the fact that, inevitably, they were constantly falling short of their goals. But they refused to be satisfied with things as they were, alerted contemporaries to the worst evils of their time, and took the first all-important steps toward improvements. Probably because women were themselves excluded from political power, they could more readily feel for those downtrodden, mistreated, and neglected by an increasingly wealthy society. In the age of rapid industrialization, ruthless exploitation, and rapid urbanization, there seemed to exist a natural affinity between reformers and women. Most of the leading female reformers were Progressives; and most of the Progressives endorsed the reforms with which women were concerned. While it is true that the vast majority of women were unaffected by all these activities and continued to be concerned mainly with domestic affairs, the changes the reformers helped to bring about in the social structure ultimately affected all women and society as a whole.

CHAPTER ELEVEN

Women in the Era of Reform

Anyone who seriously concerned himself with the welfare of American women in the early nineteenth century sooner or later had to face the hard facts concerning the woman worker. The employment of women increased steadily with the advance of industrialization. In 1870 women wage earners represented fifteen percent of the labor force, in 1900 twenty percent. Most of these women worked in the least skilled, lowest paid industrial occupations, over forty percent of them in the exploited service trades. Their wages were usually one half to one third those of men in similar occupations, as is detailed in Elizabeth Baker's *Technology and Woman's Work.*

Particularly bad were the conditions of workers in the "sweated" industries. A contemporary reports that in 1890 20,000 sewing women in New York tenements worked from eleven to eighteen hours a day at piecework rates. Agnes Nestor, who became the first female president of an AFL local union, worked for many years in a glove factory in Chicago for five cents an hour, averaging $3.00 a week.

Women and Organized Labor

Working women had been attempting to organize since the beginning of the nineteenth century. The first labor organization in the United States to accept women members on an equal basis was the Knights of Labor, founded in 1869. Women were accepted for membership both in mixed units or "assemblies" and in sex-segregated locals. In 1886, when the union reached its peak strength, it had chartered 113 women's assemblies.

A few female leaders attained local and even national leadership. Mrs. George Rodgers appeared at the General [National] Assembly of the Knights in 1886, carrying her three-weeks-old baby, the last of her twelve children. She had attained the position of "Master Workman" or chairman for the Chicago area and credited her husband with her success. "My husband always believed that women should do anything they liked that was good and which they could do well. But for him I would never have got on so well as a Master Workman."

Another pioneer trade unionist was Mrs. Leonora M. Barry, who became "general investigator" or national organizer for the Knights of Labor. A hosiery worker by trade, she had started work in a mill at sixty-five cents a week. As a trade union official she spent three years investigating conditions such as those she had known as a worker, organizing dozens of new "women's assemblies" and lecturing tirelessly to the general public. The apex of her career was passage of a factory inspection bill in Illinois that helped in curbing child labor.

In the 1890's the female membership of the Knights of Labor shared in the general decline of that organization, which was soon replaced by the American Federation of Labor (AFL).

The AFL concentrated on organizing skilled workers into craft union locals, and showed little interest in low paid, unskilled female workers. Except for occasional convention resolutions in favor of organizing women workers and the short-lived appointment of a female AFL organizer in 1892, little progress was made in this field until decades later.

An almost legendary figure among unionists was "Mother Jones." An Irish immigrant brought to this country as a child,

Mary Harris Jones grew up in Michigan, worked as a dress-maker in Chicago, taught school in Memphis, and married an ironworker and union man. In 1867 she lost her husband and her four children in a yellow fever epidemic. She became an organizer for the Knights of Labor and later for the United Mineworkers Union. A slight, motherly figure in a black bonnet, she carried all her possessions with her in her knitted shawl. She claimed that she lived wherever there was a fight against wrong. "My address is like my shoes," she declared, "it travels with me." For fifty years Mother Jones was in the thick of the bitter and often bloody struggles of mine workers. She mobilized the miners' wives for picket duty when their husbands were jailed or forbidden to picket by injunction, and once led an army of miners' wives armed with mops and brooms against deputy sheriffs with bayonets. Mobbed, beaten, and jailed, she never failed to return to the embattled mining camps and to the miners who called her "Mother."

Ella Reeve Bloor and Elizabeth Gurley Flynn were women of like caliber. Militant and deeply involved in the cause of labor for most of their lives, they were radicals who saw the advancement of women as only one necessary step in the advancement of all working people. They moved from unionism to socialism and communism, but never lost their ties with working women.

Emma Goldman, the anarchist, and Kate Richards O'Hare, the socialist and close associate of Eugene Debs, represented other strains of the radical labor movement. World War I and the postwar era separated the radicals ideologically and politically from the more moderate reformers, but in the early decades of the century radicals and reformers of every persuasion could unite around a few basic issues, among which were woman suffrage and protective labor legislation.

The National Women's Trade Union League (NWTUL). Founded during the 1903 AFL convention, the NWTUL provided a much-needed impetus toward organizing women workers. It aimed at representing working women and advancing their interests within the trade union movement; it also became the spokesman of the working woman within the woman's rights movement.

At its inception, the NWTUL was characterized by a unique and temporary cooperation in leadership between philanthropic middle- and upper-class women, and those from the ranks of labor. The organization sought to win the economic rights of women by a combination of trade union organization and political action. Its board of directors gradually brought more and more trade union women into positions of leadership. The stalwarts of reform, Jane Addams, Lillian Wald, Mary McDowell, gave way to Mary Anderson and Emma Steghagen of the shoe workers, Agnes Nestor of the glove workers, Mary Kenney O'Sullivan of the bookbinders, and Rose Schneiderman and Leonora O'Reilly of the garment workers. By 1919 Mrs. Margaret Dreier Robins was the only member of the board who was not a worker.

The NWTUL took a flexible approach to a variety of pressing problems and was active in many areas. But its main contribution remained to link working women and women interested in suffrage in a mutually advantageous alliance which did much to secure the final suffrage victory in the East.

Between 1909 and 1913 militant strikes of garment workers in Baltimore, Chicago, Philadelphia, and New York focused national attention on the horrors of sweatshop labor. The NWTUL gave active support to the strikers—raising funds, providing legal counsel, running relief kitchens, and educating and organizing the public in support of the strike. It mobilized the goodwill, economic resources, and influence of society and club women on behalf of union women and was invaluable in providing organizational continuity in the fight for protective labor legislation. The 1911 Triangle Shirt Waist factory fire in which 147 workers, most of them young girls, died because of inadequate fire escapes, overcrowding, and locked exits, awoke a shocked nation to the need for legislative protection of workers. Improved fire protection laws in New York and several other states were the direct result of the NWTUL's unremitting efforts after the disaster.

The NWTUL also helped to evolve the concept of a "living wage," which became the focus of decades of struggle for protective labor and welfare legislation. In this field women played

135

a most important and seldom recognized role. Despite the fierce resistance of employers and legislators, public support for protective legislation for women was won with the argument that the health of their offspring would be impaired unless they were protected. Once the legislatures and courts had accepted the principle of government intervention on behalf of women workers, it proved possible to win protective legislation for men as well. The 1908 *Muller* v. *Oregon* Supreme Court decision, giving judicial sanction to the regulation of women's hours of work, was a precedent-setting decision for labor and paved the way for future regulatory legislation. Minimum wage legislation had to be won in a similar manner.

The NWTUL, like the Consumers League, utilized research to bolster its arguments. It was largely through its efforts that Congress authorized a massive fact-finding investigation into the conditions of women and child workers. The nineteen-volume report by a group of experts provided much ammunition for the legislative battle. Gradually the concept that the government had a right, even a duty, to intervene on behalf of the most exploited segment of the population was accepted, to become enshrined at last in the protective labor legislation of the New Deal. The NWTUL made one of its major contributions to this process by helping to secure the establishment of

a Women's Bureau in the Department of Labor and placing two of its leaders, Mary Anderson and Mary Van Kleek, at its head. The Bureau set labor norms and goals, investigated conditions, and kept the public and Congress aware of problem areas.

High living standards for workers, dignified working conditions, social security, and protection in sickness and old age have come to be considered essentials of the American way of life. These rights and privileges were hard-won. Women, both in and out of the trade union movement, made valuable contributions to the decades of struggle for protective labor and social security legislation. In doing this, they merely broadened their traditional concern for social welfare and community building to include the most pressing problems of an industrial society.

Working women were faced with too many urgent and immediate needs to have much interest in the winning of suffrage. But all reformers who tried to change existing laws, and experienced the agonizing frustrations of dealing with a well-financed and powerful opposition, sooner or later came to see the advantages of gaining political strength by adding the votes of women to those of male reformers. Woman suffrage was seen by urban Progressives as well as by agrarian Populists as a means, not an end. They supported it because they hoped the votes of women would serve to advance other reforms.

Reform in the West

This view of woman suffrage as a means rather than an end explains one of the paradoxes which has long intrigued historians: the early passage of woman suffrage legislation in the West, rather than in the East where the suffrage movement had originated and showed its greatest strength.

The only four states to adopt woman suffrage in the nineteenth century, and the first seven to adopt it in the twentieth century, were western states. This has variously been explained by the existence of frontier democracy, by the relatively high status of women in areas where they were scarce, and by the absence of old institutions with a vested interest in the legal subordination of women. A combination of these factors was

137

"Sweatshop" labor

undoubtedly at work. But Alan P. Grimes' recent study, *The Puritan Ethic and Woman Suffrage,* has indicated that woman suffrage was never an isolated issue decided on its own merits. Rather, the use of woman suffrage as a way to gain other ends helps explain the paradoxical western development.

Wyoming.   In the 1860's Wyoming territory was opened up by railroad construction. Railroad workers were followed by miners, cattlemen, adventurers, gamblers, and saloon-keepers —a rough population out to "strike it rich" and ever ready to pull up stakes and move on to more promising bonanzas. Lawlessness flourished and was only fitfully checked by vigilantism and lynch law. The newly-formed territorial government hoped to improve community standards by attracting married householders, to whom it granted large parcels of land.

Mrs. Esther Morris, a former milliner from Oswego, New York, who had been exposed to the feminist lectures of Susan B. Anthony, thought that the situation offered a good chance for the enactment of woman's rights legislation. Her persuasiveness influenced the governor, while many of the legislators realized that the votes of women, traditional supporters of stability, would double the voting strength of the "law and order" faction. The first territorial legislature enacted a suffrage law, passed a married women's property bill, and outlawed pay discrimination against female teachers.

This astonishing victory for woman suffrage in 1859 was the first in any of the states and territories. Its immediate effect was to make the next territorial election a great deal more orderly and less fraudulent than had been the previous one. The expected shift in the relative electoral strength of the parties did not occur; it appeared that the women voters, as was confirmed by later history, split along the same lines as did male voters. However, by virtue of being voters, women were now made eligible for jury duty, and Mrs. Esther Morris of South Pass City, Wyoming, became the first female justice of the peace. On juries and in politics, women represented a strong force for law and order. Thus woman suffrage here represented not so much the working of frontier democracy but a reaction against the rowdiness and lawlessness of frontier life.

138

Utah. For quite different reasons, the territory of Utah gave women the vote in 1870. Mormon Utah was at that time threatened by the rapid settlement of the area by "gentiles"—non-Mormons—who came in the wake of the transcontinental railroad. In reaction to the pronounced distaste of the Federal Government and the rest of the nation for the Mormon practice of polygamy, the Utah government enacted woman suffrage to prove that Mormon women preferred polygamy and would vote to uphold it. This they did and, as expected, provided a counter-balance in voting strength to the—largely unmarried—non-Mormon population. To punish the Mormons, Congress abolished female suffrage in Utah territory in 1887. Later legislation outlawed polygamy and curtailed Mormon power. By 1896 woman suffrage was no longer a controversial issue in Utah; it was re-enacted and written into the state constitution, making Utah the third state to make women eligible to vote. Colorado had previously adopted woman suffrage by referendum in 1893 with the support of the People's party [Populists]. Idaho, which had a large Mormon population, followed suit in 1896.

In each of these states reformers had hoped to use woman suffrage to advance their own goals. The Woman's Christian Temperance Union (WCTU), which was strong in the western states, had been the first organization to link up suffrage with other reforms. It had also shown women that they needed the vote in order to carry out the reforms they wanted. Feminists repeatedly argued that women were and would continue to be a force for social improvement and reform. Acceptance of this assumption provided agrarian Populists and city Progressives with a common cause in the support of woman suffrage, and linked the disparate movements of West and East.

Opponents of Suffrage

Tying woman suffrage to other reforms had its disadvantages, however. The very persuasiveness of the WCTU's appeal to women drove the liquor interests into desperate opposition to woman suffrage, for fear that women would inevitably vote for prohibition. This argument was very influential with foreign-born voters who believed, with equal fervor, in the free use of wine and beer and in the sanctity of the patriarchal family. As it happened, prohibition was enacted *before* woman suffrage, and repealed by the votes of both men and women.

The pre-Civil War alliance between advocates of woman's rights and of abolition had confirmed southern politicians in their opposition to suffrage. To them, female suffrage threatened to bring with it social change, easy divorce, and a host of extremist demands. Southern suffragists accommodated themselves to these prejudices by accepting white supremacy without question. But the southern states held out against suffrage to the very end.

Southern and northern textile interests and other industrialists employing female workers at low pay feared that female suffrage would bring with it a rush of minimum wage legislation. Other business groups were driven into the anti-suffrage coalition by fears of the alliance between suffragists and social reformers. These misgivings also motivated the opposition of politicians, party machines, and entrenched hierarchies on every level of government. All feared that "the hand that rocks the cradle" might, given suffrage, also rock the boat.

This same period also saw the rise and spread of anti-suffrage movements with predominantly female membership. Their main strength was in New England, but they had organizations in twenty states. They issued literature and newspapers and lobbied to bring their argument before the public: women did not need the ballot, did not want it, and were content with their undisputed rule of the home. The effectiveness of the "antis" is debatable, but they did give legislators added arguments for delaying discussion of or decision on the issue.

All the opponents of suffrage had one thing in common—they were conservative in their social outlook. They managed to delay the advent of female suffrage by several decades, but they could not hold up the changes that were transforming American society, and with it American women. These changes, in turn, made the enactment of suffrage inevitable.

PART FOUR

The Modern Woman

In the early decades of the twentieth century women were an integral part of the upsurge of reform activity which occurred in response to the problems created by rapid industrialization and territorial expansion. Better educated than their mothers and grandmothers, twentieth-century women were increasingly impatient with the spotty progress of reforms to improve the status of women. The woman's rights movement gained momentum as increasing numbers of reformers of all kinds saw in female suffrage the cure-all for the evils of society. For a short while, this movement united women of all social classes in a common cause. World War I accelerated the entry of women into new fields of industry and created a favorable climate of public opinion, in which the long struggle for female suffrage could at last be brought to victory.

But, contrary to expectations, woman suffrage did not decisively alter the status of women in American society. The promised bloc-voting of female voters failed to materialize. Instead, class, race, and ethnic factors proved to be decisive in motivating voting behavior. American women have to this day achieved no more than token political representation.

As more and more lower-class women entered the labor market, they participated in trade union struggles together with men and benefited from trade union gains, although to a lesser extent. Wage differentials based on sex persisted, as did discriminatory hiring and promotion practices. The economic gains of the period consisted mostly in access to a larger number of low paid, low status occupations, designated as "women's jobs."

The depression wiped out whatever economic gains women had made, as men were given priority in the competition for scarce jobs. World War II seemingly reversed this trend and once again brought large numbers of women out of the home and into industry. But at the end of the war returning veterans quickly reclaimed their "rightful places" in the economy, displacing female war workers. Millions of women voluntarily retired to domesticity and war-deferred motherhood.

Middle-class women, who now had free access to education at all levels, failed to take significant advantage of it, succumbing to societal pressures regarding the proper sphere for women. Today, women are greatly underrepresented in most professional occupations. The 1950's saw a dramatically rising birth rate, earlier marriages, and the cultural acceptance of the old-fashioned view that woman's happiness was to be found in domesticity, maternity, status-seeking through consumption, and hobbies suitable to her education.

And yet the position of American women in the 1950's was dramatically different from that of their grandmothers. The changes were mostly cultural. Increasing mobility due to modern means of transportation, the persistent urbanization of American society, and the availability of birth control information had changed the sexual values of society. Reform in divorce laws, greater economic opportunities, and more lenient societal attitudes toward divorced women were reflected in rising divorce rates. For women, this meant greater freedom in the event of marital unhappiness, but it also meant greater emotional demands and psychic stress, as both marriage partners now expected to find personal fulfillment through marriage.

Due to rising educational levels, and hence more years of schooling, children spent more of their time away from the home. This fact combined with smaller family size and increased female longevity meant that for most women the childraising years occupied at most one third of their life span. Unprepared for this situation, many women faced serious adjustment problems and dissatisfaction in their later years.

Freudian psychology, as adapted in America and popularized through the mass media, dictated a subordinate position for women in society and classified those who strove for equal status and opportunities as deviant. But economic factors inexorably drove more and more women into the labor market. Today, one out of every three workers is a woman; more than half of all women workers are married. In the absence of adequate childcare and afterschool facilities, working mothers carry a double burden of work outside and inside the home. The United States falls significantly behind other industrialized nations in its provisions for the welfare of working women and mothers.

144

The late 1960's saw the rise of a new feminism, a movement made up largely of middle-class women who wished to revive the century-old struggle to achieve equal status in society. A constitutional amendment guaranteeing equal rights, an end to abortion legislation, and the establishment of more adequate childcare facilities are some of the demands raised by the new feminists.

The struggles of past generations have vastly improved the position of American women. Their life span is longer, their education better, their choices more varied, their possibilities for development greater. Yet social values, mores, and institutions lag far behind the material and economic progress made. The contributions of women have helped to build this nation —the next decades should see American women at last achieving first class citizenship.

CHAPTER TWELVE

Three Pioneers of Women's Emancipation

The turn of the century signaled the breaking down of the stability, security, and smugness of the Victorian age. In every area of life, old values were changing and people were looking for new ideas and new answers to age-old problems. Those concerned with the economic ills of society embraced a variety of social and economic reforms and focused their attention on giving women economic equality with men. Feminists saw the key to all problems of society in the enactment of female suffrage. Other women quietly and undemonstratively carved out new careers and new areas of usefulness through their personal achievement.

Three women, each of them working outside the organized woman's rights movement, had a significant impact on their time. Mary Baker Eddy, Charlotte Perkins Gilman, and Margaret Sanger were each concerned with the problems of modern society and of modern woman. All three transcended the strict limits of Victorian propriety in their personal lives. Each was divorced and remarried, each concentrated fanatically and singlemindedly on a favored cause, and each advocated views running counter to established belief and doctrine. Mary Baker Eddy defied convention and the tradition of female inferiority by founding a church, which became a large and successful institution; Charlotte Gilman formulated a sociological and philosophical attack on the economic concepts underlying the position of women under capitalism; Margaret Sanger defied law, tradition, and all notions of propriety by advocating birth control as a basic right of women. Each approached her cause from a very different point of view, but each contributed significantly toward the thinking of her time and toward changing the image of the modern woman.

Mary Baker Eddy

Very much a product of the Victorian age, Mary Baker Eddy (1821–1910) addressed herself to the problems of her time with the intellectual tools of a nineteenth-century woman. Her lack of education, her preoccupation with religion, her reliance on mesmerism and faith healing made her fairly representative of women in the earlier part of the century. So also did her long periods of hysterical illness, which produced debilitating pains, weakness, and faintness—conditions which we would today characterize as psychosomatic, but which occur with astonishing regularity in the biographies of women of Mary Baker Eddy's time.

Mary Baker's first husband died young. An unhappy second marriage to an improvident husband, who deserted her, ended in divorce. For many years thereafter Mary Baker was occupied in seeking cures for her ailments. In 1862 she was miraculously, as it appeared to her, cured by the faith healer Dr. Phineas P. Quimby, who thenceforth became her spiritual and medical mentor. She studied and practiced her "animal magnetism" cures for a number of years and incorporated many of his ideas into her own theories. After suffering a brief relapse into illness, she was cured by the application of an improved version of Quimby's methods, which became the foundation for her own religion, Christian Science.

147

From 1870 on she practiced and taught the new method and in 1875 wrote a textbook, *Science and Health With Key to the Scriptures,* which became the bible of the new religion. In 1877 she married one of her students, Asa G. Eddy; two years later the Christian Science Association she had founded became the Church of Christ, Scientist. Gifted with strong leadership and organizational abilities, Mary Baker Eddy founded a college to train adherents, attracted over sixty thousand members to her religion and, despite numerous schisms, held undisputed sway over the Boston "Mother Church" until her death. She was thus one of the few women of her age to gain not only wealth but institutional power, and was the only female founder of a successful church in America.

The metaphysical proposition, "Man is not material; he is spiritual," was extended by Mary Baker Eddy into a complete denial of the reality of matter and mortal mind. Her church teaches that the only reality is God. Hence disease is an illusion, which can be successfully overcome by prayer and faith. In this way Mrs. Eddy, who regarded herself as godlike and became a near-saint to her followers, pointed a way out of the confusion and malaise of a period of changing values. In this she addressed herself to more than the temporary social phenomenon of Victorian "female hysteria" and held out hope to all those made profoundly uneasy by the materialism of modern life and the relativism of modern philosophy.

Charlotte Perkins Gilman

In many ways, Charlotte Perkins Gilman (1860–1935) was the complete antithesis to Mrs. Eddy. She had a poor and difficult childhood; her father deserted her mother and Charlotte Perkins learned very early the need of self-reliance. Independence was, for her, nothing metaphysical; it meant first and foremost, in Susan Anthony's phrase, "a purse of her own." She saw economic independence as the foundation upon which freedom of choice rested. To Charlotte Perkins, woman's first need was to become independent of mind, self-reliant, confident, and

149

equipped to support herself. She made a fetish of mental and physical discipline, studied and exercised rigorously, and was exacting in her demands on herself and others. Characteristically, she berated herself in later life for having written only twenty-five books in forty-two years.

In her early twenties she fell in love, but her marriage to Charles Stetson was unfortunate. The life of a housewife and young mother plunged her into severe depression, which failed to respond to psychiatric treatment. A brief vacation from child and home brought her such startling relief that she decided to separate from her husband to avoid a mental breakdown. They parted by mutual consent and later divorced. Although she suffered from occasional depressions throughout her life, they never seriously threatened her mental or physical functioning. Charlotte Perkins Gilman herself pointed out that fear of losing her independence may have been the cause of her severe reaction. In line with her most unconventional attitude toward marriage, she maintained a life-long friendship with Stetson even though he married her best friend, and consented to having their daughter raised by him and his new wife. By the time of her second marriage to Houghton Gilman, a lawyer seven years her junior, her economic and psychological independence was firmly established. Her second marriage seems to have been founded on a strong and affectionate relationship of mutual independence.

Charlotte Gilman earned her living as a commercial artist, speaker, and writer. She was greatly influenced by socialism and the then current theories of evolution and sociology. She wrote several volumes of poetry and some short fiction, but most of her work was sociological. She had a life-long interest in woman suffrage, but never considered it crucial to the emancipation of women. For seven years she edited, published, and wrote most of the contributions to a monthly magazine called *The Forerunner,* which concerned itself with woman's place in modern society. She also wrote books on religion and child care and an autobiography.

She was an iconoclast even in the manner of her death. Discovering that she had incurable cancer, she determined not to

become a burden to others, and for three years was able to continue her work and activities despite the disease; when she became severely incapacitated, she ended her life in August, 1935. She left a suicide note which stated, "I have preferred chloroform to cancer."

Charlotte Perkins Gilman's most important work is her *Woman and Economics,* first published in 1898, a scathing indictment of the traditional role of women. She attacked the waste of female talents and abilities and charged that antiquated social customs were crippling women and adapting them only to life-long dependency on men. She sharply attacked the economic arrangements underlying conventional marriage and pointed out that the emancipated woman would make a better mate, wife and mother. Women were different from men, she argued, different but not inferior. Their potential must be fully utilized by society.

She never admitted any contradiction between a woman's function as wife and mother and the full development of her independence as a human being. On the contrary, she defined the true emancipation of woman as the integration of these functions, producing a fully developed human being. As a logical corollary of these ideas, she accepted work for women as a natural part of their lives and urged society to provide the services needed to enable women to combine work and motherhood. In short, she defined the emancipated woman of the twentieth century as "a mother economically free, a world-servant instead of a house-servant; a mother knowing the world and living in it."

Charlotte Gilman was well-known and widely read in her time, both in this country and in Europe. Her books ran to several editions and appeared in foreign translations; she was much in demand as a lecturer and was considered one of the most radical thinkers of her day. Ironically, after the winning of woman suffrage her work was ignored and largely forgotten. Today, when dissatisfaction with the limited achievements of the early feminist movement has inspired a new, more radical feminism, Charlotte Gilman's work speaks forcefully to the present generation. She was the first to point out that suffrage was not central to winning true equality for women and that drastic changes in the family, sex mores, and social organization were needed. Too advanced for her day, Charlotte Gilman is today seen as a pioneering leader in American social thought.

Margaret Sanger

Born in Corning, New York, the daughter of a freethinking, Catholic stonecutter, Margaret Sanger (1880–1966) born Higgins, learned early in life to associate poverty and large families. She later wrote, "Mother bore eleven children. She died at forty-eight. My father lived until he was eighty." This simple fact haunted Margaret Higgins' childhood. Although her father was a kind husband, she always felt that her mother's frequent childbearing had undermined her health. All around her she could see the connection between large families, poverty, and deprived childhood.

Margaret Higgins left home early and became a trained nurse. At the end of her training she fell in love with and married William Sanger, an architect, and for the next twelve years devoted herself to being a housewife and mother. Early in her married life she had a long bout of tuberculosis, which flared up at various times later and impeded her activities. She had three children whom she loved dearly and raised in an atmosphere of warmth and happiness. When they were old enough to be in school she returned to the job of a public health nurse, and these years spent working in the slums of New York were decisive for her later development:

> Constantly I saw the ill effects of childbearing in women of the poor. Mothers whose physical condition was inadequate to combat disease were made pregnant, through ignorance and love, and died. Children were left motherless, fathers were left hopeless and desperate, often feeling like criminals, blaming themselves for the wife's death— all because these mothers were denied by law knowledge to prevent conception.

153

> My own motherhood was joyous, loving, happy. I
> wanted to share these joys with other women. . . . Since
> the birth of my first child I had realized the importance of
> spacing babies, but only a few months before had I fully
> grasped the significant fact that a powerful law denied and
> prevented mothers from obtaining knowledge to properly
> space their families.[22]

She had witnessed the terrible effect of improperly adminis-
tered or home-induced abortions, which frequently ended in
severe illness, needless pain, even in the death of the mother.
Margaret Sanger became convinced that the withholding of
contraceptive information was a special hardship on the poor
and was, in fact, one of the major causes of poverty. It seemed
to her futile to work at relieving the effects of poverty without
touching one of its main causes. The Federal Obscenity Act and
similar New York state laws, known as the Comstock law after
their sponsor, Anthony Comstock, prevented the dissemination
of birth control information. The New York state law denied
women family planning information and forbade doctors to
dispense such advice, even in cases where the mother's health
and life were threatened by pregnancy. Margaret Sanger decided to defy this law until it could be abolished. Birth control
—a phrase she coined—became her personal crusade.

Margaret Sanger soon realized that hers was a lonely fight.
Reformers were absorbed with a variety of good causes and did
not consider changes in the Comstock law an urgent priority.
Feminists, although deeply sympathetic, advised her to wait
until woman suffrage had been enacted. Socialists and radicals
warned that only basic changes in the economic system could
bring relief for women. Not a single doctor could be found who
was willing to risk his career to give her accurate birth control
information. Her magazine, *Woman Rebel,* had a pitifully small
circulation, and she had constant trouble finding printers.
When she advocated the legalizing of birth control, the magazine was confiscated by the post office.

But Margaret Sanger persisted, and in 1914 she was indicted
for publishing "obscene" information. Although she was pre-

pared to go to jail to dramatize the injustice of the law she wished to change, she was not willing to undergo this ordeal until she had achieved her primary goal: to give American women the information they needed for scientific family planning. She evaded arrest by spending a year in Europe, where she studied contraceptive methods and government-approved family planning clinics. She learned that in Denmark and Holland family planning programs had resulted in a drastic lowering of child and maternal mortality rates. Encouraged by the success and support of European family planners and fortified by accurate medical information, Mrs. Sanger returned to the United States to find that the earlier charges against her had been dropped. A trumped-up case against her husband for violation of the Comstock law, for which William Sanger served a one-month jail sentence, focused public attention on the problem and began to change public opinion in her favor.

Mrs. Sanger published the facts she had learned and with her sister, Ethel Byrne, proceeded in 1916 to set up the first birth control clinic in America. It operated for a few weeks in the slums of Brooklyn in defiance of the law, and then—as expected —both sisters were arrested, tried, and sentenced to one month in the workhouse for violation of the Comstock law.

Both served their sentences, and Ethel Byrne conducted a spectacular hunger strike during the entire period. It almost cost her her life, but she succeeded in making their imprisonment daily front page news and in winning massive public support for their cause. The two women had the satisfaction of seeing their case lead to the passage of a law granting physicians the right to give birth control advice in cases where the health of the mother might be impaired by childbearing.

Public interest and support grew rapidly. In 1921 the first American Birth Control Conference was held. Four years later the movement became international. Educational and legal work was carried on by the American Birth Control League, and despite strong opposition, especially from the Roman Catholic Church, Mrs. Sanger had the satisfaction of seeing the dissemination of birth control information by doctors legalized in the United States in 1937.

Today Margaret Sanger is considered a great humanitarian and benefactor in countries such as India, Japan (in both of which she had a particular interest), and Puerto Rico where persistent poverty, crowded living conditions, and deprivation have made population control synonymous with economic progress. Now, when family planning is the stated goal of almost every government in the world, when the United States government is spending millions of dollars to disseminate birth control information in underdeveloped nations and among the poor in our own cities, it seems almost incredible that only fifty years ago a woman had to brave jail, exile, ostracism, and the wholesale disapproval of her contemporaries for advocating this reform.

Margaret Sanger was a fanatic and often used unorthodox methods to reach her goal. But the horror that haunted her all her life was the image of unwanted children born into families too poor to support them, of mothers looking upon motherhood as a disaster, of mothers forced to end unwanted pregnancies by illegal operations that endangered their own lives. "We want children to be conceived in love, born of parents' conscious desire and born into the world with healthy and sound bodies and sound minds." This ideal of happy child- and motherhood inspired her despite the chorus of abuse from those who could interpret her humanitarian concern only as an invitation to sexual license.

But Margaret Sanger was farsighted and bold enough to understand the full implications of her crusade. She demanded and gained for women the right to make the basic decisions which would shape their lives. Today, when the ready availability of the pill and other methods of birth control have given women a sexual freedom inconceivable in the past, the age-old role of women as passive bearers of whatever fate men decided for them is no longer defensible. Yet the old cultural attitudes toward women persist. The bitterness of this conflict can best be seen in the current controversy over reform of abortion legislation. Despite evidence of shifting ideas on the subject, most legislators still hold that childbearing is a fit subject for legislative action. Modern-day feminists hold, with Margaret

157

Sanger, that the decision to take on the responsibilities of motherhood is a personal one in which legislation has no place. This question is one which the present generation will have to decide.

As for Margaret Sanger, her impact on history may prove to be greater than that of most reformers. For she did more than reform an antiquated law and show people a way out of the cycle of poverty—she gave modern woman the priceless gift of joyous, planned motherhood.

CHAPTER THIRTEEN

The Winning of Woman Suffrage

The formation of the National American Woman Suffrage Association (NAWSA) in 1890, which unified the two branches of the suffrage movement, signaled the transition from nineteenth-century leadership to the next generation. Although the veterans were still on the scene, a new group of leaders was doing the active work. Elizabeth Cady Stanton served as president of NAWSA for its first two years, but she was absorbed in her private campaign of exposing the role of religion in keeping women suppressed. Her *Woman's Bible* served to embarrass and alienate many of the more moderate leaders from her.

At the 1892 convention Susan B. Anthony took over the presidency of NAWSA, a position she held until 1900. She was followed by Mrs. Carrie Chapman Catt, who served from 1900 to 1904, and then by Dr. Anna Howard Shaw, who held the position until 1915. During these years the organization concentrated on winning woman suffrage state by state. But a succession of hard-fought campaigns led to only two successes —in Colorado and Idaho. This period was often referred to by suffragists as the "doldrums" of the movement.

New Leadership for the Suffrage Movement

The deaths of the triumvirate of old leaders—Lucy Stone in 1893, Elizabeth Cady Stanton in 1902, and Susan B. Anthony in 1906—marked the end of an era. Old-timers were discouraged and fell by the wayside; new leadership floundered in its search for new approaches. It was a period when the majority of Americans were absorbed with a succession of economic problems, American expansion into the Caribbean and the Pacific, and the domestic problems of rapid urbanization, industrial exploitation, and agrarian stress. When measured against the plight of children laboring long hours in factories and fields, the abysmal working conditions of female factory hands, the sweatshops, and the problems of immigrants in the slums, the subject of woman suffrage seemed less urgent, less dramatic, and less appealing.

Dr. Anna Howard Shaw (1847–1919). In 1904 the presidency of NAWSA was taken over by Dr. Anna Howard Shaw. As a child, she had made the westward trek across the Michigan wilderness and suffered the hardships of pioneer life. Later she took the usual route of teaching school in order to earn money for college. She suffered bitter hardships during her years of graduate education and had to overcome the resistance of her family, her friends, and academic community in order to become a theologian and a licensed minister. During several years of pastoral work in Massachusetts, this unusual woman also completed a course at Boston University Medical School and, in 1886, earned her M.D. degree.

These experiences and her many years of work as a doctor in Boston slums gave Dr. Shaw great sympathy and understanding for the working woman and the poor. This found expression in her writing and speaking. A short, stout woman with a pleasant, outgoing personality and a fine sense of humor, Dr. Shaw was known as a superb lecturer and a powerful lobbyist. She idolized Susan B. Anthony and determined in every way to follow in her footsteps, but while Susan B. Anthony had always considered herself a revolutionary, Dr. Shaw represented the

160

An early anti-suffrage cartoon

very essence of middle-class respectability. Her eleven-year presidency of NAWSA was marked by no distinguished forward thrust, either in organizational method or political perception. As one historian of the movement has stated, she made the suffrage movement holy, and she also made it dull. Her weak leadership encouraged decentralization and gave more power to rival state groups.

Sectional differences accentuated these centrifugal tendencies. Westerners who had already won suffrage resented the directives and leadership of Easterners. Southerners insisted on working for female suffrage and for white supremacy. In an effort to win over reluctant southern politicians and voters, they pointed out that the votes of white women would serve to offset the votes of black men. They raised no objection to the process of systematic disfranchisement of black men and women through state laws.

During these years, while NAWSA persisted in a decentralized approach to suffrage, leadership and initiative shifted to the various states, bringing to the fore the organizing talent which was to revitalize the movement. Of the many dedicated

leaders, none was more significant in bringing victory to the suffrage cause than Carrie Chapman Catt.

Carrie Chapman Catt (1859–1947).   A Westerner by birth, Carrie Lane had taught school and been a high school principal in Mason City, Iowa, when she amazed her community by becoming Superintendent of Schools, the first woman to hold such a high rank in school administration. She left the job after several years to join her husband in newspaper work. Early widowhood, and first-hand experience of the trials and tribulations faced by a professional woman trying to support herself on her own, made her a devoted feminist. From the late 1880's on she worked steadily as a suffrage organizer. She played a leading part in the grueling but unsuccessful 1890 South Dakota suffrage campaign and in the three successful campaigns in Colorado, Idaho, and Utah. She toured the southern states with Susan B. Anthony in 1895 and became chairman of the National Committee on Organization, a post which brought her organizing talents to the attention of the national leadership.

In 1890 she married George Catt, a civil engineer of very liberal mind who had great sympathy for her cause. They drew up a formal contract specifying that Mrs. Catt would have several months of the year during which she could devote herself to the cause of suffrage. Since Mr. Catt's business took him out of town a good deal of the time, this unusual arrangement proved mutually satisfactory.

In 1896 Mrs. Catt presented an organizational plan to NAWSA which, besides putting the chapters on a sound, businesslike basis, mapped out a long-range strategy for victory. She regarded decentralization as a temporary necessity. Work for the state amendments was necessary in order to win the grass roots support which alone could secure a federal amendment. She told the convention:

> For a whole half century we have held special suffrage meetings with audiences largely of women. We should now carry our question into every town meeting, caucus, and primary, for it is only there that the rank and file of

162

the voters go. They won't come to our meetings. It will be of no more avail in the future than it has been in the past to send appeals to states and national political conventions so long as they are not backed by petitions from the majority of the voting constituents.[23]

Only after a number of states had accepted woman suffrage would there be sufficient congressional support for a federal amendment. "A Congressman is a green toad on a green tree, a brown toad on a brown tree," said Mrs. Catt. "He reflects his constituents." Her long-range political perspective and her practical and pragmatic understanding of political reality distinguished her from most of the preceding presidents of the organization.

In her first four years as president of NAWSA, from 1900 to 1904, Mrs. Catt was able to carry her reorganization plan into practice, but her overall strategy was not yet acceptable to the leadership. Upon her temporary retirement from national leadership she was replaced by Dr. Anna Shaw. After a brief interval of working for the international feminist movement, Carrie Chapman Catt devoted her attention to New York City.

There, several independent women's groups had earlier put new life into the old cause by adopting some of the tactics of the British suffragists and forming an alliance between trade union women and feminists. Their persistent political work was rewarded when, in 1910, the several groups united in the Woman's Suffrage Party of New York City under the chairmanship of Mrs. Catt. Under her vigorous direction a professional approach to politics was instituted. Copying the organizational structure of Tammany Hall, each assembly district was provided with a leader, each election district with a captain. These political workers were trained in schools and repeatedly visited every voter in their district. In 1913 a major campaign was launched for a New York state referendum. Twice the woman suffrage bill was presented to successive legislatures over violent opposition, and finally it was voted on in November, 1915.

The final campaign for this 1915 referendum was brilliantly directed, the most professional campaign the suffragists had ever conducted. It featured over six thousand meetings, a direct personal canvas of sixty percent of the registered voters, the distribution of three million leaflets, and a constant and concerted publicity and propaganda campaign. Imaginative promotional ideas were developed, including parades and appeals to special groups—there was a "Fireman's Day," when suffragists visited one firehouse after another, and a "Barber's Day," when women in decorated cars stopped at selected barbershops, distributed posters and campaign literature, and held open air meetings in front of the shops. In one of the huge suffrage parades five thousand schoolteachers marched, carrying blackboards on which slogans were chalked. Imaginative and unorthodox methods like these were used to keep the issue before the public eye.

Despite great efforts, the referendum secured only forty-two percent of the vote. But the suffragists met defeat like old pros. Two days after the election they called a mass meeting at Cooper Union Hall with brass band, flags, and all the paraphernalia of victory. Every county in the state was represented and with great enthusiasm over $150,000 was raised for the next campaign, which was begun then and there. The organizing effort continued relentlessly, with specific attention being given to converting the wives of Tammany Hall politicians to the cause. Over one million signatures of women in the state petitioning for suffrage spoke a language the politicians could understand. When the second referendum came up for a vote in 1917, Tammany Hall instead of opposing it took a neutral position. This change on the part of Tammany Hall was decisive in securing victory for the referendum.

The Road to Victory

The final phase of the suffrage campaign can be dated from 1912. After sixty-four years of organizational effort for woman suffrage only nine states had allowed women to vote, all in the West and controlling a total of only forty-five electoral votes.

The suffrage amendment had not been debated in Congress since 1887 and remained unnoticed and unreported in committees of both houses. Two of the parties running in the 1912 presidential election, the Socialists and Theodore Roosevelt's Progressives, endorsed woman suffrage. However, the nation continued to ignore the subject for another two years.

Prospects for passage of a federal amendment looked worse than ever after disappointing referendum campaigns in Arizona, Kansas, Oregon, Michigan, Ohio, and Wisconsin. In the last three states mentioned results were strongly indicative of fraud. It was clear that opposition to woman suffrage would mount in direct proportion to the political significance of the state. The only ray of hope was the 1913 passage, with Progressive support, of the "Illinois law," a measure which gave women presidential suffrage through an action of the state legislature. Although this first victory east of the Mississippi was encouraging, it was not followed by others. Increasingly, suffragists turned their attention to Washington where a new dynamic force within the movement had developed.

Alice Paul (1885–   ).   A Quaker and college-trained social worker, Alice Paul had in 1912 become chairman of the Congressional Committee of NAWSA. Having spent several years in England, during which time she had taken an active part in the British woman suffrage campaign and had several times been imprisoned for her part in demonstrations, Miss Paul was committed to activist tactics. She launched her campaign by organizing a suffrage day parade in Washington the day before Woodrow Wilson's inauguration. The parade was attacked by mobs and the ensuing riot was stopped only by the National Guard. The publicity helped immensely to call attention to the long-dormant issue, as did successive delegations which began to bombard Senators and the President with suffrage petitions from every state.

Miss Paul, while ostensibly still working under the leadership of NAWSA, took an increasingly independent stance. She formed a group called Congressional Union, but still retained chairmanship of NAWSA's Congressional Committee. While NAWSA advocated gradual conversion of legislators and the

President by persuasion and moral pressure, the Congressional Union took the position that power was the only language politicians understood. The party in power must be held responsible for failure to pass the federal amendment. This meant campaigning against the dominant Democratic party, even though the President was reputed to be sympathetic to the amendment and many Democrats in Congress were staunch supporters. In 1915, while both Senate and House brought the amendment to a vote and defeated it, the Congressional Union worked against the Democrats in those states where women already voted, and continued its nationwide campaign.

When Carrie Chapman Catt again assumed the presidency of NAWSA in 1915 and worked to tighten her control of all the organization's activities, including the Congressional Committee, a split between the two groups became inevitable. Miss Paul was removed from her post and the Congressional Union

left NAWSA, later becoming the National Woman's party, an organization with one single plank in its platform—the passage of the federal woman suffrage amendment.

The "Winning Plan."   When Mrs. Catt became president of NAWSA for the second time, she had an executive board of her own choosing which enthusiastically supported her approach. Shortly after her election she was made the trustee and recipient of a two million dollar legacy from Mrs. Frank Leslie, a long-time supporter, with the mandate to use the money on behalf of woman suffrage. This most encouraging and helpful gift was put to good use in the coming years.

At the September, 1916, convention, NAWSA adopted what came to be known as Carrie Catt's "Winning Plan." It was a shrewd and elaborate strategy for a relentless political drive. The NAWSA board was to lead and coordinate all state activities. Thirty-six state associations were pledged to fight to the finish to get the federal amendment passed and ratified. But before the passage of the federal amendment, it was thought necessary to win state referenda in at least one southern and one eastern state and to win partial suffrage, according to the Illinois model, in a number of states. The overall goal was passage and ratification of the federal amendment by December, 1920.

The National Woman's Party.   While NAWSA, under Mrs. Catt's experienced leadership and working within the existing party structure, set out vigorously to carry this program to completion, the Woman's Party went over to more dramatic tactics. Having worked for the defeat of Woodrow Wilson in his bid for a second term, the party proceeded to embarrass the President in every way possible during his years in office. Beginning in January, 1917, women pickets appeared at the White House and stood in silent vigil around the clock, holding up their banners. It is ironic that the picketing began at the opening session of the Congress in which the first woman member, Representative Jeannette Rankin from Montana, took her seat.

With the American entry into World War I, the Woman's Party picket banners began referring to the President as "Kaiser Wilson" and proclaimed, "democracy should begin at home." The pickets were not deterred by the denunciations of press and

167

(left) Carrie Chapman Catt
(right) Alice Paul

public, in which NAWSA joined, nor were they stopped by the threats and physical attacks of soldiers and sailors, who tore the banners out of their hands. Finally, arrests began. Within four months, 219 women from 26 states were arrested; 97 were sentenced to prison terms in the notorious Occoquan Workhouse in Virginia. Alice Paul, Lucy Burns, and several socially prominent women were mistreated in the workhouse, demanded "political prisoner" status, and finally resorted to hunger strikes. The authorities then proceeded to force-feed them, which resulted in their getting an enormous amount of publicity. The fact that the courts invalidated all the arrests and convictions a few months later helped to turn the protestors into heroines in the eyes of many, although the immediate effect of the militants' tactics was to turn a number of legislators against the cause and to reinforce the arguments of the opponents of woman suffrage. Still, the Rules Committee of the House, which had for years bottled up the federal amendment,

brought it to the floor while the demonstrations were going on. If nothing else, the militants had forced the issue out into the open in Congress.

Women and the War.   NAWSA meanwhile lent its whole-hearted support to the war effort. Carrie Chapman Catt assumed chairmanship of a woman's committee of the National Manpower Board and developed a program for the maximum involvement of women in the war effort. Women ran bond drives and did war relief work. They initiated meatless, wheatless, and butterless meals, knit huge quantities of socks and sweaters, and cut their skirts short in order to save material. Thousands donned overalls to become "farmerettes" on the nation's farm front. Women substituted for the absent men as they had in the Civil War, working as streetcar drivers and subway guards, freight handlers, tractor drivers, and mechanics. They entered fields in which they had never worked before and proved themselves capable and adequate.

Unlike leaders of the suffrage movement during the Civil War, Mrs. Catt insisted that the drive for the federal amendment must go on simultaneously with support of the war effort. During this entire period the Woman's Party tactic was to oppose the war, to burn President Wilson's speeches, to hang him in effigy, to interrupt war rallies with appeals for democracy at home, and to accuse the administration of hypocrisy in fighting a war for freedom abroad while denying women the vote.

The Final Push

The contribution of women to the war effort, their relentless pressure on Congress, and the dramatic demonstrations of the militants produced a change in public opinion. The victory of the suffrage amendment in New York state in 1917 proved crucial and was followed by passage of the "Illinois law" in a number of states. Victory was finally in sight.

On January 10, 1918, the federal amendment came up for a vote in the House. The day before, President Wilson endorsed the amendment in a private statement. For several weeks suffra-

On the march for suffrage

gists from all over the nation had been increasing their pressure on Congressmen. Every single vote counted. Every single vote must be cast. Members of NAWSA had convened in Washington and were present in the galleries of Congress. The dramatic session began when Representative Jeannette Rankin introduced the amendment. Three Congressmen came from hospitals to vote for the amendment; ailing Representative Henry Barnhart of Indiana had to be carried into the chamber on a stretcher. Representative William Jones, who had been on the West Coast, arrived at the Capitol just in time to answer to his name on the roll call; Representative Frederick Hicks of New York came from the deathbed of his wife, who was a devoted suffragist. After he had cast his vote for suffrage, he returned home to bury her. The vote was 274 in favor, 136 against—one vote over the required two-thirds majority.

The Senate Vote.   Suffragists were exultant. But victory was far from won; it would take another year and a half to get Senate acceptance and then, with only eleven states having full suffrage, ratification would take enormous work. The Woman's Party resumed its militant agitation and attacks on Woodrow Wilson; NAWSA resumed its patient and painstaking campaigning.

In September, 1918, the Senate debated the issue, and the President took the tradition-breaking step of addressing the Senate as the measure came up for a vote and endorsing the "Anthony" amendment. This was much resented, and in October the Senate defeated it by two votes. The defeat was due to opposition from a combination of the New England states and the Democratic South—a coalition of conservatism, states' rights, and possibly cotton industry interests.

NAWSA then concentrated on helping to defeat four anti-suffrage Senators. After a strenuous campaign, they succeeded in defeating two and cutting the majority of the other two. In the meantime state campaigns continued, and South Dakota, Michigan, and Oklahoma joined the suffrage list, bringing the total of suffrage states to twenty. In February, 1919, the amendment came up once again and was defeated in the Senate by one vote.

In several more months of work six more states were added to the suffrage list. President Wilson called a special session of Congress on May 20, 1919, and again asked for passage of the suffrage amendment. The House repassed the measure 304 to 89 and this time the Senate passed it too, in spite of a last desperate stand by the opposition which included a five-hour speech by Senator James Reed of Missouri. He spoke in vain; on June 4, 1919, the Senate voted 63 to 30 to submit the Nineteenth Amendment to the states.

Ratification. The opponents of the amendment then turned their efforts toward preventing its ratification. They had to find thirteen states to hold out against ratification. They knew they would have no difficulty holding the solid South, and they hoped to hold Kentucky, Tennessee, New Jersey, Connecticut, Vermont, and New Hampshire. But New Jersey ratified, followed by Kentucky in January of 1920. By then thirty-five states had ratified; only one more was needed. In all of the remaining states opposition was very strong, and their governors were opposed to passage.

The crucial decision came in a special session of the Tennessee legislature. The bill passed the state's Senate, but when it finally reached the House floor on August 26, 1920, it appeared to be short two votes. The decisive vote came from twenty-four-year-old Harry Burns, the youngest member of the House. His mother was a staunch suffragist and had written to her son, "Hurrah! And vote for suffrage and don't keep them in doubt. I noticed some of the speeches against. They were very bitter. I've been watching to see how you stood but have noticed nothing yet. Don't forget to be a good boy and help Mrs. Catt put 'Rat' in Ratification."

Harry Burns voted yes, and by a 49 to 47 vote of the House of Tennessee the Nineteenth Amendment became law. American women had won the suffrage.

CHAPTER FOURTEEN

The Twentieth-Century Woman

The winning of suffrage, which had occupied the energies and hopes of several generations of American feminists, soon proved a disappointment. Women voted, but they did not vote in recognizable blocs, nor did they use their votes for the betterment of society. They voted, by and large, along party lines, as did men. Women voted, but they did not succeed in winning political power. In numbers they were the majority of the population; in political representation they remained a negligible minority.

Women in Government

In the Ninetieth Congress (1967–68) women occupied only 2 percent of the seats, with one woman Senator, Margaret Chase Smith, and 11 Congresswomen. In other years there had been as many as 20 women in Congress. Of the total one third had succeeded to their husbands' unexpired terms, and most of these were then unsuccessful in their bid for election in their own right. Between 300 and 400 women served in state legislatures during any one year, while as many as 900 had appointive positions in the states. In addition, about 30,000 women served in county and municipal positions, among them two dozen or fewer women mayors. The figures are hardly impressive, considering that women hold 52 percent of the votes and outnumber men 100 to 97 in the population.

In federal appointive office the lone female Cabinet member only served to prove the general rule that top governmental and business posts were reserved for men. The first female Cabinet member was Frances Perkins, who as Franklin D. Roosevelt's Secretary of Labor built a distinguished record. The position of treasurer of the United States has consistently gone to women since Georgia Neese Clark first held it under President Roosevelt. A few female ambassadors, a handful of female judges in the federal courts, and the customary female vice-chairmen of both major parties give no more than token recognition to the actual strength of women voters. The appointment by President Kennedy of the President's Commission on Status of Women under the chairmanship of Eleanor Roosevelt represented a recognition on the highest level that equality of treatment and opportunity for women was far from achieved.

Female Governors.   There have been three female state governors, all of them serving only as a result of their husbands' previous tenure of the office. Nellie Ross of Wyoming succeeded her husband, who died in office in 1924, served one term, and was defeated for re-election. She later became a four-term director of the Mint. "Ma" Ferguson of Texas ran for governor as stand-in for "Pa," James Ferguson, who had been impeached. Her campaign slogan was "Two Governors for the Price of One." Her 1924 election victory, despite her political inexperience, was a defeat for the state's Ku Klux Klan; her record within the state was creditable, although she was never taken seriously outside of Texas. Defeated in her bid for re-election, she was elected for a second term in 1932. In a similar spirit, Mrs. Lurleen Wallace successfully ran for the governorship of Alabama in 1966 after her husband was prevented by state law from succeeding himself. A shy woman, Mrs. Wallace never seemed to feel quite comfortable in her assumed role, but loyally held to her post even during her severe terminal illness in order to further her husband's political ambitions.

These three governors simply exemplify the traditional subordinate role of women in politics brought up to date. The wives of Presidents, Senators, and candidates for office have traditionally performed an important public function on behalf of their husbands, as have the wives of important leaders in the business world. Yet, it must be stressed, theirs is entirely the public role of a wife, not that of a political figure who happens to be a woman. The distinction is important, because the measure of the advance made by women in our society is not so much their progress as wives as their progress as persons.

Anna Eleanor Roosevelt (1884–1962).   A woman who transcended the traditional role of the wife and became a significant political figure in her own right was Anna Eleanor Roosevelt.

As the wife of Franklin Delano Roosevelt and the mother of six children, she performed all the traditional duties of a governor's wife and a First Lady. Her keen social awareness was put into her husband's service after his attack of polio in 1921, when she became his researcher and his contact with people he could not physically reach.

Participating in Democratic party politics on a state and national level, Eleanor Roosevelt soon became a political force in her own right. A columnist, writer, and speaker, she was active in many fields of reform and became the target of much hostile criticism, largely because of her unusual energy and her deep concern for the underprivileged of the nation. Upon her husband's death she was appointed delegate to the United Nations General Assembly. As chairman of the United Nations Commission on Human Rights from 1946 to 1953 she realized her lifelong goal of working for equality and peace on a world scale. Hers was traditional feminine concern functioning on the highest political level.

Local Political Activities

With the winning of suffrage the feminists had abandoned their militant action-oriented organizations. The League of Women Voters (an outgrowth of NAWSA) saw itself as a strictly nonpartisan group dedicated to clean government and political education. Women continued after 1920 to exert considerable influence for community betterment and social reforms, but these energies were channeled largely through the traditional community organizations, PTA's and women's clubs, rather than through political organizations. Within the political parties women remained for a long time in separate divisions, mostly occupied with their traditional fundraising role. Only after World War II did women begin to make their way up in the power structure of the political parties.

The Continuing Fight for Equality.   Shortly after passage of the Nineteenth Amendment various reforms in discriminatory laws gave women more nearly equal legal status with men. But

Anna Eleanor Roosevelt

in the majority of states discriminatory legislation remained on the law books, covering such areas as labor, divorce, juror qualifications, property, and inheritance. The Woman's Party continued to focus on the legal discrimination against women. It sought passage of an equal rights amendment to the Constitution, which would wipe out all discriminatory legislation and make men and women equal before the law. The measure never received the widespread and passionate support the Nineteenth Amendment had received, and ran into opposition from those who feared it would wipe out all protective labor legislation favoring women. The issue has recently gained fresh life due to the agitation of new feminist organizations.

World War II. During World War II millions of female war workers replaced the men at the front in shipyards, war industries, and in the domestic economy. Curiously, this fact had no impact on their post-war political influence and standing. But it did affect greatly the goals and expectations of those women who for the first time in their lives were offered well-paying jobs, free child-care centers, and training opportunities for skilled employment. Yet so strong was the power of traditional ideas concerning woman's role that there was little effective opposition when returning veterans displaced female war workers in the economy. "Rosie the Riveter" was told to go home where she belonged and to produce babies, not ships. She did just that, as can be seen from the post-war baby boom.

Yet women had made great strides during the 1920's and 1930's in regard to other aspects of their lives. These were first evident in a revolution of manners.

Social Equality. Nothing could be a more dramatic symbol of the changes in woman's position than the transformation of the whale-boned, corseted, bustled, ruffled and petticoated Victorian into the bare-kneed, short-skirted flapper of the 1920's with her bobbed hair. With a change in dress came a new attitude toward the female body. Outdoor exercise, competitive sports, and modern dance soon made the sickly, frail, Victorian ideal of femininity look as outmoded as the horse and buggy.

The physical freedom of dress was only the outward mark of greater social equality and freedom. A number of taboos were

177

World War II worker

rapidly discarded. Women now smoked and drank in public and entered, with very few exceptions, any public facility; they asserted their right to set their own standards of sexual behavior and happiness; and, like their male contemporaries, they took to the automobile and the highways. The greater mobility and economic and physical independence thus gained largely removed women from the strict parental restraints which had governed them in previous centuries.

In the world of sports, the achievements of swimming champions like Annette Kellerman and Gertrude Ederle and tennis stars like Helen Wills led to the acceptance of women on a par with men. When Althea Gibson, who had been the first of her race to participate in the Forest Hills tennis championships, went on to become the first black women's singles title holder at Wimbledon, England, in 1957, she struck down another time-hallowed discriminatory barrier.

In the newest sport, flying, women have performed creditably. Amelia Earhart's achievements dramatized the new sense of equality women experienced in the twentieth century. Today, although many women practice flying and parachute jumping as a sport and several thousand hold pilot licenses, there are as yet no female commercial pilots; nor have women been permitted to enter the field of space exploration.

Culture. The cultural activities of modern women have reflected the drastic changes in morals and mores which have taken place in this century.

In the dance world, Isadora Duncan revolutionized the concept and style of modern dance with her barefoot dancing and her insistence on self-expression and feeling translated into body movement. Her Bohemian life and romantic death in an open automobile, strangled by the folds of her long scarf which caught in the spokes of a wheel, became symbols for the generation of the 1920's of the prototype of the emancipated woman. Ruth St. Denis, Martha Graham, Katherine Dunham, and others elevated American dance to the first rank in the international art world and helped to create a new ideal of American femininity, which combined grace and freedom, self-expression and natural beauty.

The "emancipated" woman of the 1920's

The theater has always been one field in which women have had equal employment opportunities with men, producing numerous great and celebrated actresses and opera singers. In the beginning of the twentieth century, however, women entered the field of theatrical direction or production for the first time. Eve LeGallienne and Margaret Webster are outstanding among the pioneers in this field.

In literature women continued their best-seller tradition with such perennial favorites as Mary Roberts Rhinehard, Edna Ferber, Pearl Buck and Frances Parkinson Keyes. By the 1930's women were firmly established on the literary scene. Among the memorable names are the short story writers Dorothy Parker and Katherine Anne Porter, the playwright Lillian Hellman, and the journalist Dorothy Thompson. Anne Morrow Lindbergh brought the question of woman's role before millions in *Gift from the Sea,* as Betty Friedan would later do from an entirely different viewpoint in her *Feminine Mystique.* Gwendolyn Brooks became the first black writer to win the Pulitzer Prize for poetry. Rachel Carson's influential *Silent Spring* continued the Dorothea Dix tradition of reform by exposé, with the difference that the modern reformer was no longer simply an outraged idealist, but a highly trained scientist of acknowledged professional repute.

With the lessening of social restraints, the twentieth-century woman could freely enter literary fields of a more social character, writing plays, screenplays, and scripts for television, and could find ready acceptance for her work.

In the mass media, women made their mark as newspaper columnists, offering advice and counsel on the woman's pages and, later, even in feature columns. Women reporters and journalists were long confined to "women's interest topics," but have lately broken out of this narrow field into general journalism. In radio and television women were to be found mostly as glamorous "personalities" and have only recently been slowly integrated in other aspects of programming. They are now to be seen also as weather reporters, interviewers and, occasionally, newscasters, but the important fields of news analysis and political commentary remain male preserves.

180

(bottom left) Jeanette Rankin, politician
(top left) Margaret Mead, educator
(top right) Jane C. Wright, physician
(bottom right) "Babe" Didrickson Zaharias, athlete

In music, where major orchestras had long been bastions of male supremacy, the twentieth century brought a gradual integration of female performers in most orchestras. Even the previously sacrosanct domains of composition and conducting gave way to the achievements of a handful of female pioneers.

Science. The second and third generations of college-trained women produced many scientists. Florence Rhena Sabin, a graduate of Smith College and holder of an M.D. degree from Johns Hopkins, specialized in zoology and in 1905 became the first woman professor at Johns Hopkins Medical School. From 1925 to 1938 she was a full professor at the Rockefeller Institute of Medicine. She became the first woman elected to life membership of the National Academy of Science. The Director of the Rockefeller Institute declared in 1930 that she was "the greatest living woman scientist." Her specialty was the investigation of the lymphatic system, blood vessels, and the origin of red blood cells.

Other women honored for their outstanding work in medicine have been Dr. Helen Taussig, who pioneered in surgical operations on "blue babies," and Dr. Jane C. Wright, a black physician, director of cancer chemotherapy at New York University Medical Center and Associate Dean of New York Medical College.

There is in the twentieth century no field of scientific endeavor in which women have not participated and to which they have not made outstanding contributions. Among physicists the work of Lise Meitner, the great German-born physicist who contributed to the development of nuclear fission and the A-bomb, is particularly noteworthy.

Among the great anthropologists of the twentieth century are Ruth Benedict and Margaret Mead. The latter has served as curator of ethnology at the Museum of Natural History, director of the Columbia University Research in Contemporary Culture, and professor of anthropology at Columbia. Margaret Mead's academic distinctions are matched by her work as a popularizer of anthropological knowledge. As a columnist in women's magazines, in which she discusses our own and other cultures, she particularly emphasizes the role of women.

There are women to be found in almost every field of the technical sciences. A remarkable personality is Lillian Muller Gilbreth, the first woman in the field of scientific management. Married to Frank Gilbreth, a motion-study specialist, she utilized her training as a psychologist, applying it to engineering and management studies. She combined a scientific and business career with the raising of twelve children, a feat that was accomplished largely by the application of scientific management methods to the Gilbreth home. She has recently served as chairman of the Department of Public Relations of Newark College of Engineering, and as member of many government commissions.

The advance of women into every aspect of business, even up to the managerial and executive level, has progressed steadily. The recent seating of the first woman on the Stock Exchange— Mrs. Charles Ulrick Bay, chairman of the board and president of A. M. Kidder & Co.—has pointed up the fact that there are hardly any inviolably male preserves left in American society. Passage of the Civil Rights Act of 1964, Title VII of which forbids sex-based job discrimination, highlights the progress made, at least in statute and law.

But Mrs. Bay remains very much an exception. Much has been made of the power of women as "holders of the nation's purse strings." Indeed, the millions of American housewives do decide whether to buy one brand of peanut butter or another, one pair of jeans or two, one manufacturer's cosmetics or another. For the market, these are important decisions; but the decisions which are essential to the economy of the nation are not consumer decisions, they are production decisions. The big corporations, the basic industries, the utilities, the banking and finance establishments of the nation are run and controlled by men. Even those wealthy women who inherit their husbands' large fortunes have their money managed by men. The occasional exception only proves the rule. Thus woman's purchasing power is consumer power, small-scale and limited in its economic impact. Men control the major economic policies.

Employment statistics point this up sharply. Ever since the 1920's there has been a steady upsurge in women's employment. Currently 36 percent of the work force are women; that is, one out of every three workers is a woman. According to the Bureau of the Census, women now can be found in virtually every occupation listed. But the fact remains that the vast majority of working women are to be found in the occupations they have traditionally held. In 1960 80 percent of all employed women were to be found in these traditional occupations: clerical and sales work, service occupations and domestic service, and factory and farm work.

Figures on women's earnings illustrate the vast inequality of their economic position—the median income (meaning half of the total earned above and half below this figure) of full-time wage earners in 1968 was: white men, $7870; black men, $5314; white women, $4580; and black women, $3487. Women earned considerably less than men in every kind of occupation, and they were predominantly employed in low-paying occupations. Only 13 percent of all women were to be found in professional occupations; in those nursing and teaching (with the exception of college teaching) predominated, employing 59 percent of all professional women. Women were grossly underrepresented in law, medicine, engineering, and science. Only 6 percent of medical doctors and 4 percent of lawyers and judges were women. This reflects the regression in the graduate education of women, who in the 1920's earned almost 15 percent of the nation's doctoral degrees, compared with only 11 percent in the 1960's, although 40 percent of the undergraduates in the country were women. These figures emphasize the gap between the rapid and ever-expanding legal gains of women and their actual patterns of choices. Where past generations had placed the greatest stress on removing legal and social obstacles from the paths of women, expecting that these achievements would lead to actual equality of opportunity, the present generation is more aware of the real obstacles and considerations faced by women in making their life choices.

This awareness has, in recent years, led to the growth of a new feminist movement. The reform wing of this movement is embodied in NOW (National Organization of Women), an activist civil rights organization which uses traditional democratic

184

Women demonstrators in support of
Women's Liberation movement

methods for the winning of legal and economic rights, attacks mass media stereotypes, and wants equal rights for women in partnership with men. The organization and others like it cooperate with the more radical groups in coalition activities, such as campaigns for abortion law repeal, expanded childcare facilities and passage of the equal rights amendment. The more radical and youthful Women's Liberation groups support most of these goals with vigor, and at times with unorthodox means, but are essentially dedicated to making basic changes in the institutions of society.

Women's Liberation groups have engaged in a broad variety of activities. They publish magazines, newsletters, articles, and books, and run feminist theatre, film, and study groups. They have demonstrated on behalf of imprisoned Black Panther women and other female prisoners. They have interrupted the Miss America pageant, burned their bras and girdles in public, and broken up television shows and legislative hearings with similar tactics. Women's Liberation group members have organized women workers in business offices, worked with neighborhood women for better health and childcare facilities, and organized women's caucuses in various professional organizations. They have examined the hiring and promotion practices

of colleges and professions, gathered and published statistics on wage discrimination, instituted lawsuits, and demanded changes in college curricula, including the establishment of departments for feminist studies.

What all new feminists have in common is anger at the continuance of unequal economic status for women, determination to incorporate sexual equality into all the institutions of our society, and an awareness that the subordinate position of women in many areas of life adversely affects them psychologically and hinders their achievements. New feminists do not wish to turn women into men, as some of their detractors believe. They simply deny that the obvious biological differences between the sexes necessarily mean that men and women should function differently in other aspects of life. They consider most of the attributes we describe as sex differences not biological, but cultural in nature—that is, acquired through childhood training and societal indoctrination. Therefore, new feminists wish to see changes not only in the laws and institutions of society, but in the values, psychology, and family life of both men and women. They are asking for a re-examination of our most basic assumptions about the role of women in society and are insisting that the idea of feminine equality be applied in childraising, education, culture, sex, and family life. Only when that is done, they believe, can legal and economic equality for women become a reality.

EPILOGUE

The modern American woman's opportunities are limited only by her ability to take advantage of the many choices open to her. No longer faced with the age-old conflict between career and motherhood, she can and does combine marriage, motherhood, and work. Three out of five working women are married; one out of every three mothers with children under eighteen is working. Because they share in the general poverty of their group, the choices for most black women are more limited. Black mothers are more likely than white to continue working after their children are born; the explanation is purely economic —twice as many black mothers as white are poor.

All American women now live longer (the life expectancy of a baby girl is seventy-four years; in 1900 it was forty-eight years); they marry younger and they have their children earlier. By the time her youngest child enters school, the average American mother is thirty-two years old. The modern woman's lifespan now extends far beyond the childbearing stage. Even the millions of mothers who prefer to devote their full time to their children while they are young will have the opportunity (and the likelihood) of working at other periods in their lives. For most women, a maximum of twenty-five years is devoted to childraising, leaving some thirty years free to perform other social functions. Statistics bear this out: the life-work span of the average American male is forty-three years; that of unmarried women forty years, of married women without children thirty-one years, and of all women twenty-five years. The vast majority of women will work sometime during their adult lives.

Whether the American woman chooses to work or to devote her time to community and volunteer services during the years not given over to child-raising and nurture, she now has a vast range of choices open to her. Many women see their lives as falling into a number of distinct phases, with shifting emphases. Childhood and education occupy the first two decades, motherhood and child nurture the next, some sort of training and part-time or full-time work fill the next two decades, while retirement provides a chance for community service. Career-oriented women place greater emphasis on the continuity of their working life and make full use of community facilities, such as nursery schools and day care centers, to allow them to combine motherhood with a career.

The 35,000,000 American women who devote their full time to homemaking are, however, still the majority. Their lives, too, have been enriched by new opportunities, their burdens have been eased by technological innovations and a vast array of auxiliary housekeeping services such as dry cleaners and laundromats, their standards of homemaking and child care have been immeasurably raised by their own education and the wealth of information available to them through the mass media. Following in the old tradition of American women, the housewife is the mainstay of community organization, the fundraiser for churches and charitable groups, the concerned guardian of community educational facilities and social services.

In the changed and smaller American family, which has gradually given over many of its functions to the community, child nurture and consumption provide the main focus. The housewife is the central figure in the field of consumption, the family purchaser and treasurer. As the chief consumer the American housewife is wooed, cajoled, besieged, and beleaguered by the conflicting claims of the manufacturers of commodities which she is urged to purchase. While the actual power of the consumer to influence economic decisions may be debated, our society certainly stresses this aspect of woman's role above most others. Here, too, the woman has a number of choices open to her. She may simply make consumer decisions between one product and the other, or she may join with others for protecting consumers, enforcing higher standards, improving products and services, and correcting abuses.

Today, educational opportunities for girls are on a par with those available to boys. While thirty-three percent of all women over eighteen graduate from high school, as against twenty-five percent of all men, only one percent of women gets more than five years of college education, as against four percent of men. The relatively low percentage of women in the top level professions stems from a variety of causes. Chief among these is the fact that most women wish to marry and become mothers, and that the consequent interruption of their careers is more damaging in the professional fields than it is in semi-skilled or less skilled occupations. Lack of adequate childcare facilities, rigidity of training and employment patterns, and the high cost of domestic servants also tend to restrain the career opportunities of professional women. Tradition and male prejudice are undoubtedly factors in a number of fields, but factors which can be overcome by persistence and institutional reform. The restraints now existing are so much less formidable than those which faced nineteenth-century women that they undoubtedly can and will be overcome when women have a sufficiently strong desire to do so.

In the fields of child and maternal welfare and protective legislation much remains to be done. In this area, the United States is falling behind most of the industrialized capitalist nations of the world, and some of the socialist countries as well. Even our great advances in health standards are being undermined. In infant and maternal mortality rates the United States has long since slipped from first place. Most industrialized nations provide paid maternity leaves and job guarantee for maternity leaves, by law or by union contracts. Only two of our states and Puerto Rico provide for paid maternity leaves.

Similarly, most industrialized nations have long recognized the importance of childcare centers both to mothers and children, and have made them widely available. Childcare centers at public expense were first established in this country during World War II, but were quickly cut back after the end of the war. Now only a few states run such centers, restricted to the children of working mothers. There are inevitably long waiting lists.

Sweden and other Scandinavian countries furnish paid vacations for housewives and many countries give cash family allowances to all families, a measure which immensely benefits large, poor families. All these measures and many others are social reforms which, in this country, await the dedicated efforts of men and women of this generation. Compared with the gains already made by our forefathers, these reforms are relatively minor. Our abundant society can well afford them.

The young woman in America today, relatively unhampered by custom and restrictions, enjoys unparalleled opportunities for developing her talents and abilities. She may choose among any number of totally different life styles. She may, if she wishes, play different roles in different periods of her life. Her opportunities for self-fulfillment have never been greater; and, paradoxically, her dilemma has never been more profound. The multiplicity of choices of necessity means conflicts and doubts, uncertainty and the potential for error. But that is the price that must be paid for freedom.

The rich contribution made by women to American development and growth, to the opportunities and freedoms we prize as the "American way of life," is worth treasuring and defending. The challenges of the future are great enough to absorb the talents, creativity, and energies of all Americans—women and men.

Bibliography

General

Beard, Mary, ed., *America through Women's Eyes* (New York: Macmillan Co., 1934)

Beard, Mary, *Woman as Force in History* (New York: Collier Books, 1962)

Botkin, Benjamin A., *Lay My Burden Down* (Chicago: University of Chicago Press, 1965)

Dexter, Elizabeth Anthony, *Career Women of America: 1776–1840* (Francestown, New Hampshire: M. Jones Co., 1950)

Dexter, Elizabeth Anthony, *Colonial Women of Affairs* (Boston: Houghton Mifflin Co., 1931)

Flexner, Eleanor, *Century of Struggle: The Woman's Rights Movement in the United States* (Cambridge, Mass.: Harvard University Press, 1959)

Gilman, Charlotte Perkins, *Women and Economics* (New York: Harper and Row, 1966)

Grimes, Alan Pendleton, *The Puritan Ethic and Woman Suffrage* (New York: Oxford University Press, 1967)

Holliday, Carl, *Woman's Life in Colonial Days* (New York: Frederick Ungar Publishing Co., 1922)

Kemble, Frances Ann, *Journal of a Residence on a Georgian Plantation* (New York: Alfred A. Knopf, 1961)

Klein, Viola, *The Feminine Character* (New York: International University Press, 1949)

Kraditor, Aileen S., *Ideas of the Woman Suffrage Movement, 1890–1920* (New York: Columbia University Press, 1965)

Kraditor, Aileen S., *Up from the Pedestal* (Chicago: Quadrangle Books, 1968)

Leonard, Eugenia A., *The Dear-Bought Heritage* (Philadelphia: University of Pennsylvania Press, 1965)

Lerner, Gerda, "The Lady and the Mill Girl: Changes in the Status of Women in the Age of Jackson," *Midcontinent American Studies Journal,* X #1 (Spring 1969) pp. 5-15.

Martineau, Harriet, *Society in America,* 2 vols. (New York: Saunders and Otley, 1837)

Massey, Mary Elizabeth, *Bonnet Brigades* (New York: Alfred A. Knopf, 1967)

Morris, Richard, *Government and Labor in Early America* (New York: Columbia University Press, 1946; Harper Torch Books, 1965)

Morris, Richard, *Studies in the History of American Law* (New York: Columbia University Press, 1930)

O'Neill, William L., *Everyone Was Brave: the Rise and Fall of Feminism in America* (Chicago: Quadrangle Books, 1969)

O'Neill, William L., *The Woman Movement: Feminism in the United States and England* (London: George Allen and Unwin Ltd.; New York: Barnes and Noble, 1969)

Riegel, Robert E., *American Feminists* (Lawrence: University of Kansas Press, 1968)

Sinclair, Andrew, *The Emancipation of the American Woman* (New York: Harper and Row Publishers, 1965)

Spruill, J. C., *Women's Life and Work in the Southern Colonies* (Chapel Hill, N. C.: University of North Carolina Press, 1938)

Stanton, Elizabeth C.; Anthony, Susan B.; and Gage, Matilda J.; *History of Woman Suffrage,* 6 vols. (New York: Fowler and Wells, 1881–1922)

Biography and Autobiography

JANE ADDAMS

Addams, Jane, *Twenty Years at Hull House* (New York: Signet, 1960)

Lasch, Christopher, ed., *The Social Thought of Jane Addams* (New York: Bobbs-Merrill Co., 1965)

Linn, James Weber, *Jane Addams* (New York: D. Appleton-Century, 1936)

MARY ANDERSON

Anderson, Mary, *Woman at Work: The Autobiography of Mary Anderson as Told to Mary N. Winslow* (Minneapolis: University of Minnesota Press, 1951)

SUSAN B. ANTHONY

Anthony, Katherine, *Susan B. Anthony* (Garden City, N. Y.: Doubleday and Co., 1954)

Dorr, Rheta C., *Susan B. Anthony: The Woman Who Changed the Nation* (New York: Frederick A. Stokes Co., 1928)

IDA WELLS BARNETT

Duster, Alfreda M., ed., *Crusader for Justice: The Autobiography of Ida B. Wells* (Chicago: University of Chicago Press, 1970)

MARY McLEOD BETHUNE

Holt, Rackham, *Mary McLeod Bethune: A Biography* (New York: Doubleday and Co., 1964)

Sterne, Emma Gelders, *Mary McLeod Bethune* (New York: Alfred A. Knopf, 1957)

ELIZABETH BLACKWELL

Hays, Elinor Rice, *Those Extraordinary Blackwells* (New York: Harcourt Brace, 1967)

ANNA ELLA CARROLL

Greenbie, Marjorie B., *My Dear Lady, The Story of Anna Ella Carroll, The "Great Unrecognized Member of Lincoln's Cabinet"* (New York: Whittlesey House, 1940)

CARRIE CHAPMAN CATT

Peck, Mary Gray, *Carrie Chapman Catt* (New York: H. W. Wilson Co., 1944)

LYDIA MARIA CHILD

Meltzer, Milton, *Tongue of Flame: The Life of Lydia Maria Child* (New York: Thomas Y. Crowell Co., 1965)

DOROTHEA DIX

Marshall, Helen E., *Dorothea Dix* (Chapel Hill, N. C.: University of North Carolina Press, 1937)

MARY BAKER EDDY

Peel, Robert, *Mary Baker Eddy: The Years of Discovery* (New York: Holt, Rinehart & Winston, 1966)

CHARLOTTE FORTEN

Forten, Charlotte, *Journal: A Free Negro in the Slave Era* (New York: Collier Books, 1961)

MARGARET FULLER

Stern, Madeleine B., *Life of Margaret Fuller* (New York: E. P. Dutton and Co., 1942)

Wade, Mason, ed., *The Writings of Margaret Fuller* (New York: Viking Press, 1941)

CHARLOTTE PERKINS GILMAN

Gilman, Charlotte Perkins Stetson, *The Home: Its Work and Influence* (New York: McClure Phillips, 1903)

Gilman, Charlotte Perkins Stetson, *The Living of Charlotte Perkins Gilman* (New York: Appleton Century, 1935)

Gilman, Charlotte Perkins Stetson, *Women and Economics: A Study of the Economic Relation Between Men and Women as a Factor in Social Evolution* (Boston: Small Maynard, 1898) Paperback (New York: Harper & Row, 1966)

SARAH AND ANGELINA GRIMKÉ

Grimké, Angelina Emily, *Letters to Catherine E. Beecher, in Reply to an Essay on Slavery and Abolitionism, Addressed to A. E. Grimké.* Revised by the Author. (Boston: Isaac Knapp, 1838)

Grimké, Sarah Moore, *Letters on the Equality of the Sexes and the Condition of Woman; Addressed to Mary Parker, President of the Boston Female Anti-Slavery Society* (Boston: Isaac Knapp, 1838)

Lerner, Gerda, *The Grimké Sisters from South Carolina: Rebels Against Slavery* (Boston: Houghton Mifflin Co., 1967)

FLORENCE KELLEY

Goldmark, Josephine, *Impatient Crusader* (Urbana: University of Illinois Press, 1953)

MARY LYON

Lyon, Mary, *The Life and Labors of Mary Lyon* (New York: American Tract Society, 1885)

LUCRETIA MOTT

Cromwell, Otelia, *Lucretia Mott* (Cambridge: Harvard University Press, 1958)

ELIZA PINCKNEY

Ravenel, Harriet H., ed., *Eliza Pinckney* (New York: Charles Scribner's Sons, 1896)

ELEANOR ROOSEVELT

Roosevelt, Eleanor, *The Autobiography of Eleanor Roosevelt* (New York: Harper Brothers, 1958)

Roosevelt, Eleanor, *You Learn by Living* (New York: Harper Brothers, 1960)

ERNESTINE ROSE

Suhl, Yuri, *Ernestine Rose and the Battle for Human Rights* (New York: Reynal and Co., 1959)

MARGARET SANGER

Sanger, Margaret, *Margaret Sanger: An Autobiography* (New York: W. W. Norton and Co., 1938)

Sanger, Margaret, *My Fight for Birth Control* (New York: Farrar and Rinehart, 1931)

Kennedy, David M., *Birth Control in America: The Career of Margaret Sanger* (New Haven and London: Yale University Press, 1970)

ELIZABETH CADY STANTON

Stanton, Elizabeth Cady, *Eighty Years or More* (London: Fisher and Unwin, 1898)

Lutz, Alma, *Created Equal, A Biography of Elizabeth Cady Stanton* (New York: John Day, 1940)

DORIS STEVENS

Stevens, Doris, *Jailed for Freedom* (New York: Boni and Liveright, 1920)

LUCY STONE

Hays, Eleanor, *Morningstar, A Biography of Lucy Stone* (New York: Harcourt Brace, 1961)

HARRIET BEECHER STOWE

Fields, Annie, ed., *Harriet Beecher Stowe: Life and Letters* (Boston: Houghton Mifflin Co., 1898)

Wilson, Forrest, *Crusader in Crinoline: The Life of Harriet Beecher Stowe* (New York: J. B. Lippincott Co., 1941)

MARY CHURCH TERRELL

Terrell, Mary Church, *A Colored Woman in a White World* (Washington, D.C.: Ransdell Publishing Co., 1940)

SOJOURNER TRUTH

Gilbert, Olive, *Narrative of Sojourner Truth, A Northern Slave* (Boston: The Author, 1850)

HARRIET TUBMAN

Bradford, Sarah, *Harriet Tubman, The Moses of Her People* (New York: Corinth, 1961)

EMMA WILLARD

Lutz, Alma, *Emma Willard, Pioneer Educator of American Women* (Boston: Beacon Press, 1964)

FRANCES WILLARD

Earhart, Mary, *Frances Willard, From Prayers to Politics* (Chicago: University of Chicago Press, 1944)

FRANCES WRIGHT

✓Baker, Paul R., *Frances Wright, Views of Society and Manners in America* (Cambridge: Harvard University Press, 1963)

Perkins, A. J. G. and Wolfson, Theresa, *Frances Wright, Free Enquirer* (New York and London: Harper and Brothers, 1939)

Group Biography

Bacon, Martha, *Puritan Promenade* (Cambridge: Houghton Mifflin Co., 1964)

Dannet, Sylvia, *Profiles of Negro Womanhood* (Chicago and New York: Educational Heritage, Inc., 1964)

Douglass, Emily Taft, *Remember the Ladies: The Story of Great Women Who Helped Shape America* (New York: G. P. Putnam's Sons, 1966)

Ross, Nancy W., *Westward the Women* (New York: Alfred A. Knopf, 1944)

Thorpe, Margaret Ferrand, *Female Persuasion, Six Strong-Minded Women* (New Haven: Yale University Press, 1949)

Yost, Edna, *Women of Modern Science* (New York: Dodd Mead, 1959)

Education

Bernard, J., *Academic Women* (New York: Meridian, 1966)

Cross, Barbara, ed., *The Educated Woman in America* (New York: Teachers College Press, Columbia University, 1965)

Ginzberg, Eli and Yohelem, Alice, *Educated American Women: Self-Portraits* (New York: Columbia University Press, 1966)

Newcomer, Mabel, *A Century of Higher Education for American Women* (New York: Harper and Brothers, 1959)

Woody, Thomas, *A History of Women's Education in the United States,* 2 vols. (New York: The Science Press, 1929)

Working Women

Abbott, Edith, *Women in Industry* (New York: D. Appleton and Co., 1918)

Andrews, J. B. and Bliss, W. D. P., *Report on Condition of Woman and Child Wage-Earners in the United States,* 19 vols. Document # 645, 61st Congress, 2nd Session (Washington, D.C.: Government Printing Office, 1910)

Baker, Elizabeth, *Technology and Woman's Work* (New York: Columbia University Press, 1964)

Klein, Viola and Myrdal, Alva, *Women's Two Roles, Home and Work* (London: Routledge and Kegan Paul Ltd., 1956)

Komarovsky, Mirra, *Blue Collar Marriage* (New York: Random House, 1964)

Rainwater, Lee; Coleman, R. P.; and Yancey, W. L., *Workingman's Wife* (New York: MacFadden, Bartell Corp., 1962)

Women Today

Bird, Caroline, *Born Female, The High Cost of Keeping Women Down* (New York: David McKay Co., Inc., 1968)

Friedan, Betty, *The Feminine Mystique* (New York: W. W. Norton and Co., 1963)

Lifton, Robert J., ed., *The Woman in America* (Boston: Houghton Mifflin Co., 1965)

Kanowitz, Leo, *Women and the Law: The Unfinished Revolution* (Albuquerque: University of New Mexico Press, 1969)

Millett, Kate, *Sexual Politics* (Garden City: Doubleday and Co., 1970)

The President's Commission on the Status of Women, *American Women* (Washington, D.C.: Superintendent of Documents, 1963)

Carson, Josephine, *Silent Voices: The Southern Negro Woman Today* (New York: Delacorte Press, 1969)

Hacker, Helen, "Women as a Minority Group," *Social Forces,* XXX (Oct. 1951)

Mead, Margaret and Stern, Bernhard J., "Woman, Position in Society," *Encyclopedia of Social Sciences,* XV, pp. 439 ff.

Potter, David M., "National Character" in Edward Saveth, ed., *American History and the Social Sciences* (New York: Free Press of Glencoe, 1964), pp. 427-448

Women's Bureau, Department of Labor, *Handbook on Women Workers* (Washington, D.C.: Superintendent of Documents, 1965)

Footnotes

To retain their flavor and veracity, all citations from historical documents retain the original spelling and punctuation.

1. South Carolina and American General Gazette, March 27, 1776, as cited in Julia C. Spruill, *Women's Life and Work in the Southern Colonies* (Chapel Hill, N. C.: University of North Carolina Press, 1938), p. 182.

2. Harriott Horry Ravene, *Eliza Pinckney* (New York: Charles Scribner's Sons, 1896), p. 56.

3. Elizabeth Ellet, *The Women of the American Revolution* (New York: Baker and Scribner, 1848) as cited in Mary Beard, *America Through Women's Eyes* (New York: Macmillan, 1934), p. 81.

4. Jane Swisshelm, *Letters to Country Girls* (New York: J. C. Riker, 1853), p. 78.

5. E. C. Stanton, S. B. Anthony, M. J. Gage (eds.), *History of Women Suffrage* (6 vols.; New York: Fowler & Wells, 1881), I, p. 514.

6. Andrew Sinclair, *The Better Half: The Emancipation of the American Woman* (New York: Harper and Row Publishers, Inc., 1965), p. 205.

7. Abigail Scott Duniway, *Pathbreaking: The Story of a Pioneer* (Abbott, Kerns and Bell, 1914), p. 7. Reprinted by permission of Agency Lithograph Company.

8. *Ibid.,* p. 10.

9. Harriet Martineau, *Society in America* (2 vols.; New York: Saunders and Ottley, 1837), p. 158.

10. Frances Ann Kemble, *Journal of a Residence on a Georgian Plantation in 1838–1839,* ed. by John A. Scott (New York: Alfred A. Knopf, 1961), pp. 229-231.

11. *Ibid.,* pp. 240-241.

12. Mary Boykin Chesnut, *A Diary From Dixie,* ed. by Ben A. Williams (Boston: Houghton Mifflin Co., 1961), pp. 21-22.

13. Stanton, *et al., History of Woman Suffrage,* Vol. I, p. 116.

14. Dorothea L. Dix, *Memorial to the Legislature of Massachusetts* (Boston, 1843). Old South Leaflets, Vol. VI, No. 148.

15. *Ibid.*

16. Stanton, *op. cit.,* Vol. I, p. 70.

17. As cited in: Rheta Childe Dorr, *Susan B. Anthony: The Woman Who Changed the Nation* (New York: Frederick A. Stokes Co., 1928). Copyright, 1928, by Rheta Childe Dorr. Reprinted by permission of J. B. Lippincott Company.

18. Stanton, *op. cit.,* p. 431.

19. Parthenia A. Hague, *A Blockaded Family* (Boston: Houghton Mifflin Co., 1888), pp. 261-265.

20. Katherine M. Jones (ed.), *Heroines of Dixie* (New York: Bobbs-Merrill, 1955), p. 122.

21. Jane Addams, *Newer Ideals of Peace* (New York: Macmillan, 1907), p. 182.

22. Margaret Sanger, *My Fight for Birth Control* (New York: Farrar and Rinehart, 1931), p. 44. Reprinted by permission of Holt, Rinehart & Winston, Inc.

23. Mabel Ward Cameron (ed.), *The Biographical Cyclopedia* (3 vol; New York: The Halvard Publishing Co., 1924), I, p. 79.

INDEX

203